the
synchronicity
of LOVE

STORIES THAT HEAL, TRANSFORM, AND AWAKEN

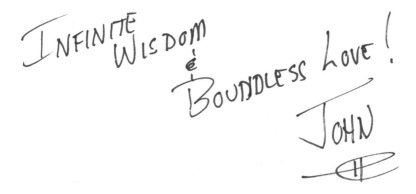

INFINITE WISDOM & BOUNDLESS LOVE!

JOHN

JOHN DAVID LATTA

Edited by Laurie Knight

An Imprint for GracePoint Publishing (www.GracePointPublishing.com)

GracePoint Matrix, LLC
624 S. Cascade Ave
Suite 201
Colorado Springs, CO 80903
www.GracePointMatrix.com
Email: Admin@GracePointMatrix.com
SAN # 991-6032

A Library of Congress Control Number has been requested and is pending.

ISBN: (Paperback) 978-1-955272-14-8
eISBN: 978-1-955272-15-5

Books may be purchased for educational, business, or sales promotional use.
For bulk order requests and price schedule contact:
Orders@GracePointPublishing.com

Praise for *The Synchronicity of Love*

John has found something remarkable: a quiet careful humbleness that a lot of people who write spiritual books often don't seem to possess! So many people nowadays try to make a living from workshops and have made a career out of awakening. That seems to drive how they present themselves to the world. This book is not that. It's wonderful, genuine, deep, and when I say "ordinary," I mean that in the very best sense of the word. There is no pretense of grandeur, no tackiness, just a genuine desire for self-understanding, and a confession of remarkable experiences with Kundalini energy! He's written some of the best descriptions of this that I've read anywhere. Please do yourself a favor and pick up a copy; it will bring some magic into your life for sure.

Chandira Hensey

John's raw, authentic sharing of his journey is compelling. You sink in and immediately identify with all he is BEing in his 3D persona. Then comes a slow, ecstatic, painful, awe inspiring, and magical journey of self-discovery. In each story, we immediately transport into his world through word illustrations that draw us into his experience. His evolution in consciousness is easy to identify with and inspiring.

Teresa Wornstaff
Collaborative Leadership Advisor

Is the heart center really the key to unlocking synchronicity? John tells us that limitations fall away when we embrace love, because love is the connective fabric that unites everything in existence. This collection of stories superbly sketches the multi-faceted mosaic that is the life of a spiritual seeker as it meanders through snippets of family life, dreams, nuggets of wisdom, encounters with a variety of teachers, mystical experiences, musings, and more. As I read these stories, they touch a place deep within me that reminds me, this is my life too—multi-faceted and satisfying in ways that are often hidden from view. It is a deeply satisfying read, gently and light-heartedly revealing wisdom without being pedantic or didactic. I thoroughly enjoyed it and will be sure to dip into it again and again, for a quick hit of whatever I might need in the moment!

Amena Siddiqi, PhD

How beautifully John has crafted the path to the Heart Center and its attributes. To feel it, to know it, and to practice it is one thing but to articulate it with the seduction that John has, I should think anybody who reads this book would want to join in this exploration. Sensitive people have not often had place in the business world. Now they do. John's book is the link.

In service to the Heart Center,
Jacqueline Bayne

The bite-sized stories present a mixture of wonderfully beautiful and mystically creative imagery, moments of belly-laughing humor, and countless seeds of ancient wisdom followed by supreme spiritual awakening. This book has something for everyone and is an absolute gem! "Losing My Head" was one of the many bite-sized stories in John's book that sparked in me a powerful inner realization (about the value of letting go). John's stories are short, but clearly powerful and with so much inherent wisdom about life and the whole spectrum of human and **spiritual** experience. Every time I read them, I notice feeling energetically cleansed, more content, and honestly just more Self-aware.

Kelsey Latta
CEO – Harmonee Dream

The Synchronicity of Love is an incredible memoir told through dreams and stories that will amaze and inspire you. Each dream or story springs forth from a question, from a deep curiosity and seeking that seems to remarkably magnetize the most powerful experience possible to bring forth the most astounding insights and revelations. True to his generous and authentic nature, John shares both the struggles and joys of living a more conscious, balanced, and intentional life during a highly transformational twenty-year period. He awakens layer after layer, creating a page-turning energy that will fully engross you. Like gems, his stories contain tips for healing and pain relief, for releasing attachments, for trusting the flow of life, for shifting one's perspective through song and mantra, and much more! John is both a brave soul seeker with many lifetimes of wisdom, and a regular guy with normal fears, who dared to open himself up to an "unmistakable life." I highly recommend you dive into this book NOW!

Melissa Wadsworth
Author of *Collective Manifestation:*
Heart-Centered Blueprints for Creating Intentional Community

The Synchronicity of Love comes to me as a rich anecdotal, and vulnerable memoir about life with spirit. Each read is like sitting with a good friend while they share their most intimate, poignant, elevating, and meaningful teachings in life, leaving me feeling lifted with each retelling. The book is written with self-effacing humility, gratitude, and wonder that repeatedly says, "I am as I am." It informs and reminds me that others, though their journey and perspective are unique, also experience dark periods, doubts, and challenges and how life can support us in the most unexpected and magical ways.

Rick Humphrey
Senior Data Analyst, T-Mobile

This book revels in brilliant possibility. John artfully showcases countless personal experiences that challenge his state of awareness. No matter the result of the experiences, he makes sure to value the process, and offers the reader wise tools to do the same in their own lives. His views and insights are sweeping and vast. He is grounded in the unknown and thrilled when the dots are connected. Either way, this book reminds you that are not alone in your spiritual journey and no matter what you know or don't know, there is inherent value in it all. Put this book on your bedside, close your eyes, flip to a page, and let the love and synchronicity inform you.

Alexandra Folz, MSN, Intuitive
Author of *The Heirloom*

It was like a tuning fork calling me to remember my way, my connection to love and spirit. A call to honor the love, compassion, and beauty in my life. That through experiencing and overcoming one's physical, emotional, and soulful wounds, one gains the gifts of healing, compassion, intuitive insights, and a closer connection to the spirit world. I highly recommend *The Synchronicity of Love.* I am sure you will enjoy John's collection of inspiring spiritual and practical insights, questions, poems, remedies, and stories that will call you to remember and embrace deeper your own spiritual path, your own best self, and the magnificent sun and love which shines in your heart.

David Krause
IT Business Intelligence and Healthcare Management

Be wary dear reader, one may ask "Why did I pick up this book?" The ultimate synchronicity here is when one learns John's lessons might well be one's own.

Christine David
University Lecturer at National
Research University, Higher School of Economics

To Wendy, thank you for being the miracle that blessedly and unexpectedly walked into my life.

To Eric and Kelsey, I am so grateful to be your father, and I am so thankful for all the adventures we shared together.

To Brugh, the Heart Priest, who taught me how to be love and in doing so renovated my entire life.

CONTENTS

Foreword

I first met John Latta in 2009. I liked him immediately. He was humble, smart, and very present as we conversed. It was obvious that he was an eager explorer of psycho-spiritual matters. He read all the important books about spirituality and had studied with several teachers. At the same time, he was a grounded family man who also owned a successful business.

He wanted to consult with me, a teacher of Transpersonal and Spiritual Psychology. This is consciousness work, which includes the areas of dreams, intuition, creativity, the imagination, spirituality, energy healing, psychological process, meditation, synchronicity, and more. Often it is simply called personal or inner work.

In this book, John vividly shares his experiences of exploring these subjects. He writes about his many first-hand experiences in an honest way, with an open mind and excitement. I was drawn into his written experiences and could sense the emotions and sensations that he shared. This is good writing!

John has written in a creative experimental form; he gifts us with his actual experiences and his insights. He gifts us further with fascinating dreams and interpretations, and then he even takes a portion of those dreams and constructs fictional stories around them. One may think that he should have written in the usual progressive way, but no, John's exciting storytelling gives us a taste and feeling of his explorations.

My favorite story of his is a dream in which John is transformed into a salmon. He sheds his clothes and dives into the river, feeling his strong fish body come alive. His powerful tail propels him around rocks and rapid waters. He is a male with long teeth and a cruel, curved snout. As he swims upstream with the throngs of fish, he knows his purpose is singular. His dream is full of rapture and gratitude.

The ability to transform into an animal form is known to many indigenous shamans. Their consciousness in the animal can see or predict weather or when it's best to plant crops, as well as other things. The salmon are fighting to propel themselves over small rapids, heading upstream where they will spawn. This takes tremendous fortitude and intention, and when John dreams this, those qualities are strengthened in him.

Today I know John as a friend and fellow teacher and group facilitator. I hold the image of him in his welcoming home and his large, lush property with dozens of people who have come for an evening of community and spiritual upliftment. The gathering is named Something True. John starts the process with an invitation to join hands and have a moment of silent meditation. "Who wants to share?" he asks. One by one, people speak their truth, whatever they wish to share, anything at all. The process continues, with the rest of the group witnessing and appreciating whatever the speaker presents. Late into the night people of all ages are uplifted with the privilege of speaking their truth and relating to other speakers.

How healing, nurturing, and inspirational each of these meetings is. As facilitator, John holds the container for others to share their own experiences of vulnerability, creativity, intimacy, and more.

Read this book. It is a wonder. I can't praise it enough. The tone is beautiful, and the entire book is exquisitely inductive. Full of imagery, and full of heart—raw and honest. It is the finest offering of first-person stories that I've read in my many years of psychological and spiritual study.

I will leave it to you to discover what the title means. Synchronicity. Love. Both the words and the book invite you into explorations that can transform your life.

Carolyn Conger, PhD, Clinical Psychology
International consultant, spiritual teacher, and author of
Through the Dark Forest

Note to the Readers

Unconditional love.

In 2002 I embarked on a path of unconditional love via heart-centered meditation. I threw myself into it with a sincere earnestness. What happened? A lot! But mostly there were four things:

- I, as I knew myself to be, grew exponentially.
- I had access to more "resources."
- I experienced more synchronicity.
- I seemed to get more with less effort.

Of course.

Embarking on a sincere and earnest path of unconditional love would produce more personal growth, more resourcefulness, more synchronicity, and more support. Why? Because love embraces all. It connects all. It embraces everyone and everything. By stepping into love and embracing love and indeed in *becoming* love, it follows quite naturally that one's sense of self begins to grow and expand because love is wholeness itself.

Embrace love, and you become more whole. You, as you know yourself to be, become larger and larger and larger. You become more. You see more. You experience more. You become aware of more. Limitations start to fall away, and miracles abound. And because love connects everything, as you grow into love, there is this strange sense that you are also swept up in the flow of love—which is the flow of life.

You, as you know yourself to be, change, change again, and then change some more.

You grow, grow some more, and then grow even more.

Your desires change, change again, and then change some more.

Effort and accomplishment are somehow easier and more supported.

One's desires go from a myriad of things to a single-focused and sincere desire to be in alignment with love. It feels like desires move from "not my will, but love's will."

This book is full of stories about what happened to me when I threw myself into love with sincerity and earnestness. During the time in which all these stories took place, I had a moderately consistent practice of heart-centered meditation. This practice consisted of placing my hands over my heart chakra (about an inch above where the ribs come together in the center of one's chest) with reverence and then inviting in unconditional love. In short, it was a volitional change in my usual day-to-day consciousness. I would sit in this state for about twenty minutes once or twice per day. The feeling was one of immense gratitude, and it felt like my entire physiology was thanking me profusely for doing this.

The function of the heart center is unique in that its job is to love and therefore it unites all things. It unites all the upper and lower chakras. It unites Heaven and Earth, the human with the divine, the masculine with the feminine, yin and yang, dark and light, body and mind, soul and spirit.

By spending time in the heart center with a sincere earnestness, I grew and experienced myself becoming more whole and more resourceful, and this growing resourcefulness was immensely helpful in life, in relationships, and in business, and it was often unexpectedly surprising as I experienced more and more "impossible" miracles.

At my core, I am a practical person—one friend calls me an "everyday mystic"—and I'm happy with that. From the point of view of wholeness and unconditional love in the heart center, I seemed to love the glories of various spiritual experiences and the practical responsibilities of raising kids, relating to my wife and others, having a job, and paying the bills. All of it. This fit me best. I truly am walking a middle path, or the middle way Home.

The stories I share here are mostly of a wide variety of true real-world experiences from which I learned and grew. But I also share many of what I call inner experiences. These experiences include encounters with what felt like inner teachers and dreams, which also helped shape me. In short, I have been transformed by both inner teachers and outer teachers alike.

I present the stories in a loose chronological order so that you can see how I grew step by step from all the inner and outer teachers and experiences. Many of the stories are shared in present tense so that you might more readily immerse yourself into them. In some cases, I chose to add my own reflections or insights from the stories, and in some cases, I simply let the stories stand alone.

As I am a person who learns best from real-life examples, it makes sense that I would write a book full of my own true experiences. But I also wrote a few poems and some fictional stories, which for me are still essentially true stories. They reveal patterns at play that were revealed in the writing—some of which were at play when I wrote those pieces, and some of which would blossom in the future. As time has gone by, the fictional stories no longer feel like fiction at all, and I learned just as much from writing them as I did from any other type of real-world experience. But if you want to know the true stories from the fictional ones, I do my best to note which is which.

My hope is that you enjoy the stories and my insights. But, even more than that, I hope you can take what I've shared here and apply it experientially in your own life. In my case, choosing unconditional love in the face of fear, choosing compassion in the face of judgment, choosing forgiveness in the face of condemnation, choosing healing for myself and others rather than causing further wounds, choosing to fully accept others as they are instead of always trying to change them, and choosing to trust life with a deep and sincere surrender rather than fighting with life—all of this has created a sort of endless series of miracles in my life wherein things just started to flow easier, and statistically improbable "coincidences" and synchronicities started to happen with ever greater frequency. The line between what is and is not possible becomes blurred in seemingly miraculous ways. Love and synchronicity go hand in hand.

The stories in this book are acts of grace, creativity, exploration, discovery, and are also full of seeds. Seeds of transformation, healing, awakening, and wisdom that took root in me were nourished and would eventually bear fruit in their own time. The stories are purposefully short and intended to simply plant seeds of healing, transformation, and awakening.

There are more than one hundred stories here, covering a wide variety of subjects. And yet, every single one of these stories is also a love story.

1

Three Seeds

For most of my adult life I was a man who passionately loved many things. I loved football and basketball and played them well into my fifties. I loved camping and road trips and fly fishing. I was competitive and successful in my career. I was intelligent and driven with lots of energy.

I was a husband and a dad who passionately loved his wife and his two children. Every day off was an adventure or a road trip—camping, fishing, traveling, exploring, hiking, swimming, and skiing. My kids were active in sports, and I loved coaching their teams.

I never expected things to change nor was I seeking change.

But, man, things can turn upside down in a hurry.

My wife got cancer. It was a sudden thing. She had noticed that she was losing hair and asked me to go with her to see a dermatologist. When we arrived, the doctor expressed concern over a small lump on my wife's thyroid gland. He quickly sent us to another doctor. This second doctor appeared gravely concerned. In what felt like mere minutes, my wife was in tears and getting a needle biopsy. We were told that she likely had a tumor on one side of her thyroid gland and that the half with the lump would be removed and that she would spend the rest of her life with half a thyroid gland, which, we were assured, was no big deal. She was still young, healthy, took good care of herself, and could survive the rest of her life with half a thyroid with no problems.

So, we waited a week for the results of the biopsy. When we got the results, they were not good. It was a fast-growing, highly malignant cancer, and surgery was scheduled immediately. They went in and unfortunately had to remove the entire thyroid gland and some lymph nodes. My wife would have to take a synthetic thyroid hormone for the rest of her life. There were follow-up treatments of radioactive iodine to kill any traces of the cancer and what might have been left of her cancerous thyroid gland. These required her being sequestered in a hospital room for weeks at a time with no visitors. (Radioactive iodine is deadly to healthy thyroid glands so my wife's exhalations, sneezes, and coughs were potentially harmful to others.)

After my wife's surgery and recovery, she was a changed person. I noticed that she began reading different types of books—about life and death and God—subjects that frightened me. I'd been a devout anti-spiritual and anti-religious person since my early teens.

I am thirteen years old. My mother, father, brother, sister, and I are walking to church. It is a beautiful sunny morning. As we approach the church, I notice my mother does not have her head covered. In our Catholic Church tradition, a woman is supposed to cover her head when entering church. My mother always wore a white lace doily on her head. I alert my mother that her head is not covered and that this is a sin. She informs me that the church has changed the rules and that it is now OK for a woman to enter and attend church without her head covered.

I am shocked. I thought that the rules had been clearly laid out in the Bible by God. There is a wound here akin to discovering there is no Santa Claus. It was not God but man, fallible man, making these rules. I stop going to church and spend the next thirty years antagonistic toward all religions and spiritual practices.

My wife is quiet and keeps much of what she is feeling and thinking to herself. I am not a good person to be speaking to about death and God. I understand hard work, strategy, accomplishment, competition, passionate play, and fun. I understand the language of argument and logic. But I manage to keep death and God at bay, so I do not know how to speak of them.

As my wife is changing, so am I.

I had worked hard in my career as a grocery store manager in a large thriving eighty-store regional chain. We lived in a big house in a nice neighborhood and had managed to save a lot of money. I had also started a business on the side that was thriving nicely. When the company I was working for was sold and then sold again, everything changed. It was no longer a great place to work. The business I was running on the side was growing like crazy, so I took the leap, left my secure career, and began running my new business full time.

But things went south fast. I lost all our money. In less than two years, we were over $500,000 in debt. I had $250,000 in personal credit card debt alone. I had to sell half of my company, but even that only made a moderate dent in all the debt. I was lost in epic fear and had no tools to cope. And in the middle of it all, my wife found someone else and moved out to start a whole new life.

And so, my happy life was crumbling. I was suddenly a single dad with custody of my two children, ages nine and eleven, and over my head in crushing debt. There was rage, fear, and grief so deep I could not even touch it.

To make it even worse, it felt like death was stalking me. I had developed an epic fear of what felt like oblivion. What would happen to me after I died? Would I just disappear? Forever? *Forever?* It was torturous and relentless—like the mind forever trying to solve infinity. I could not accept nor wrap my head around *oblivion* and *forever.*

I could not get this fear out of my head. In the rare moments when I was home alone, I was often in tears. I had no one to turn to. I did not meditate. I never prayed. I did not talk to God. I did not go to church. I had no friends or family I thought I could talk to about this, nor did I think that talking to someone would even help. So, I found myself alone, consumed with an epic fear of death and oblivion. Forever. I hid and cried alone. Terror stalked me every step of the way.

I lost nearly twenty pounds. I was already lean and athletic, so losing any weight at all was unusual. But the epic terror of oblivion, the fear that I was going to have to go bankrupt and start over, and the grief and fear I felt raising my kids alone had created an adrenaline monster that was consuming me.

I had never been a failure, at least not in any significant way. I knew what I wanted, and I went for it and usually got it. I didn't know *how* to be a failure. Suddenly, I was a bad husband, a bad father, and a bad businessman—not to mention a grown man who was terrified of death. Until that point, I had not truly had to face any real adversity. I realized then, I had it in spades. Death was stalking me, financial ruin was stalking me, raising my kids without the support of their mother at home terrified me, and, without knowing it, a midlife crisis was shrouding me.

I knew how to use anger and the energy it provided, and I was determined to be a freaking great dad. I didn't know if I could possibly save my company, but I would give it every effort. Protect my kids. Save my company. Saving John from his fear of death would come later.

I knew a couple who had saved their marriage with therapy and sought their help. They connected me to their therapist, and I began seeing her at once. (She would later note that I looked like a skinny, scrawny wreck.) Devastated by the circumstances that had befallen me, I had turned into a gaunt skeleton. I was five foot eleven and weighed only 145 pounds.

Eventually, I settled down just a bit. My company stopped bleeding cash. The kids seemed to be adjusting to our new life far better than I. I kept a solid routine. I kept coaching my kids in sports and trying to be as involved in their lives as possible. I did not date. There was no sign I would ever actually be able to get out of debt completely, but somehow, I was able to continue making the minimum payments on all my credit cards. I got good at playing the system. I applied for new low-interest rate cards and used the cash they let me borrow to pay off other high-interest rate cards.

I started to make peace with what felt like the shame of being a failure. I attended a divorce-recovery workshop and met a whole lot of people who had stories just like mine: "Gosh life was so good, and then all this shit happened out of nowhere, and suddenly now I am divorced."

But I still had not made peace with Death.

Over the course of many years, prior to my divorce, I had read and reread Michael Crichton's book *Travels*. This was Crichton's sort of autobiography. I felt like he and I saw the world in much the same way. Like me, he too was intelligent and dismissive of religion and spirituality. But Crichton went through a transformative crisis as well and came out of it determined to experience life differently—to try to directly experience things he feared or resisted and decide for himself what it all meant. So, Crichton finally broke down and attended a two-week spiritual retreat in the desert led by Dr. William Brugh Joy (known to his community simply as Brugh). Crichton wrote about his experiences there and titled the story "Cactus Teachings." For a person who was devoutly logical and anti-spiritual, I found it unusual that I must have read his story about his experiences at the retreat at least a hundred times.

I am lying on my bed. The kids are about to come home from school. I am reading Michael Crichton's story "Cactus Teachings" again. Something compels me to toss the book aside, run downstairs, and go to the internet to see if this Brugh Joy guy is still alive and if he is still teaching. It is twenty years after Michael Crichton attended, and I am not optimistic. But there he is on the web, apparently alive and well, and I see he is teaching a "Foundational Conference." Although I still have over six figures in credit card debt, I sign up immediately. It costs nearly $3,000. I assure myself that if I go bankrupt that *the extra $3,000 won't really matter. I see on his website that he promises the conference will be "life renovating." Those words hang in the air. They are magnetic. I need this. It is a lifeline.*

In the following weeks, I am genuinely scared. And excited. Given my immense distrust of all things religious or spiritual, I am depending on Crichton's description of Brugh as a super intelligent "somber medical man" and not some charismatic guru. I really have no expectations other than the life renovation part.

So, in June 2002, I fly to the high desert in Southern California for my ten days with Brugh. As the plane touches down in Ontario, California, I notice that the woman sitting next to me is reading Brugh's book *Joy's Way*. I am shocked. I look her over. *She looks normal.* I ask if she is going to see Brugh Joy, and she says yes. We both carefully check each other out. She is a grandma from Kalispell, Montana. She looks "normal." We both have a laugh and relax. A lot. We join a couple of other "normal" people in a van headed for Brugh's retreat in the mountains. I relax some more.

This was the very beginning of what was to be an extraordinary number of coincidences that I prefer to call synchronicity that seemed to defy mathematical possibility and would continue for years afterward to the present day.

The retreat is focused on the heart center and unconditional love, and I'm desperate to have my life "renovated." We stay in small cabins out in the desert high in the San Bernardino Mountains, and my roommate is a younger man named Dan. He's cool. He's athletic and adventuresome like me and is working on a degree in Chinese medicine. We bond instantly.

I share my story around my recent divorce. That my wife moved out and left me for another man to start a whole new life. That I was teetering on bankruptcy and raising our two kids without the support of their mother at home. I am still angry, full of rage and fear. I am mad at my wife for running away when things got tough. I am secretly envious of her breaking away for a fresh start in life and leaving me with all the debt and enormous responsibility. I am still in rage and denial, and it feels to me like she had coldly abandoned our children. I grieve for them daily. I am still stuck at home dealing with friends, family, and neighbors, and I feel shame and embarrassment around them. I just want to hide. I don't like people knowing my problems or even admitting that I have any problems.

But Dan coolly tells me that five years earlier, his own wife was previously married and was unhappy in her first marriage, and then she left her husband for Dan. Dan's wife had children by her first husband and now they were now Dan's stepchildren. Dan says there isn't a day that goes by that his own wife doesn't feel pain and guilt over leaving her husband for Dan, and she feels enormous pain for how she thinks it has affected her children.

Dan then assures me that my ex-wife is in pain too.

Given that my wife left me for another guy on the rebound, it suddenly occurs to me that my roommate is the "other guy." *What a strange coincidence*, I think. What are the chances that I go to my first ever spiritual retreat and my roommate is the "other guy"? I am here for "life renovation" but had not planned on anything like this.

I've never been truly open with another person, but in the spirit of unconditional love here at this retreat, we share deeply with each other. Dan shares that he wants to leave the marriage he is in now, but his wife's children love him and have bonded with him. He says he should never have married his wife when she was on the rebound, and they were both so young. He is feeling immense guilt, pain, and remorse.

So, the woman who walked out on her husband and her kids is suffering. And now the "other guy" (my roommate) is suffering too. That had never occurred to me.

As the conference begins, we are paired up with partners. Mine is Lisa, a gal about my age from the Midwest. I like her, and we seem to click. But then I find out that after the retreat she is considering walking out on her husband and kids! Unconditional love or not, I am having a difficult time with this!

So, my roommate is the "other guy" in a relationship where a woman walked out on her husband and kids to be with another guy. And now my partner here is planning to leave her husband and kids when she gets home! I can't believe it! I have an excellent math mind—very good at calculating probabilities—honed from years in business management and years of pouring over the Daily Racing Form at the horseraces. The chances of both things happening in a group of just thirty people from all over the world blows my mind. This is *not* what I expected nor what I especially wanted on my first ever spiritual retreat!

The next day, Lisa openly shares with the group that she is considering leaving her husband and her children so that she can pursue her soul's journey. Again, I feel the anger and judgment arise. I keep thinking, *She is so SELFISH. How could she do that to her children?!* I fear for her kids and the pain it would cause them.

Lisa shares that she never really got to have a childhood, that she was the eldest among all her siblings and recruited at a young age to be a co-parent. She's been a sort of selfless martyr her entire life and is tired now. Brugh calmly says to our group that if a man were to walk away from his family to pursue his soul's journey, society would find that somewhat acceptable. But if a woman were to do it, she would be damned forever.

I feel it in me . . . the desire to damn Lisa (and my ex-wife) forever. Yet . . . compassion, love, and forgiveness welled up in me as well. My roommate, Dan, is in pain. His wife is in pain. Lisa is in pain. My ex-wife is probably in pain. I am in pain. I can feel myself backing off just a bit and letting go of judgments. Hearing Dan's story, his wife's story, and Lisa's story, it becomes harder and harder for me to stay angry and judge them.

And my wife: she had just survived a sudden serious cancer scare prior to her leaving. She must take a synthetic thyroid hormone for the rest of her life, or she dies. How did that experience affect her and the choices she made? I was probably not the easiest man to be living with—I was always on edge, freaking out about what seemed to be insurmountable debt, yearning to be out of debt and for my old secure job back, and running around in tears behind closed doors in abject fear of death. I had a role to play in all this drama too.

This was the first time in my life I had experienced such meaningful and statistically improbable "coincidences." There are many words used to describe such experiences—*miracles, coincidences, serendipity,* etc. I like the word *synchronicity.* It would be years before I started to make the connection between surrendering judgments, old habits, and old beliefs and choosing to sincerely seek love, compassion, and forgiveness, and how, combined, they seem to create more and more magical synchronicity in my life.

I forgave my ex-wife. I forgave myself. I forgave Lisa. I never saw Dan again, but Lisa and I became good friends. My ex-wife and I ended up making the most of a difficult situation. We worked together on behalf of the kids, and while the custody arrangement was a bit unusual (I had custody and she had the kids every other weekend and some weeknights), we ended up getting along very well.

Brugh had talked about how all of us "carry stones" and that it is good to set them down.

I could have lashed out at Dan and Lisa. I could have stayed stuck in my anger and judgment I had toward my ex-wife. I could have carried these stones for the rest of my life.

I chose not to.

When the retreat ends, I have not had much in the way of spiritual experiences. I go home and still grieve, suffer, and struggle, although the weight of it all seems lighter. But three seeds are planted in me at the retreat that continue to bloom and grow.

One is compassion and the knowing that being human often entails great suffering, and that rather than judging another person, it is far more helpful, meaningful, and fulfilling to try to stand in their shoes to try to see as they see, and to try to feel what they feel.

The second is wisdom and that, if I can stand back just a bit from my own suffering, I can catch a glimpse of a bigger, more magnificent picture at play.

The third is the immense power of unconditional love and that, in choosing to enter it, to embrace it, and to be embraced *by* it, an endless stream of what feels like statistically impossible "miracles"—both large and small—is unleashed in one's life and what one believes is possible and impossible is forever changed.

2

Birth of the Dreamer

Not long after my retreat in the desert with Brugh in 2002, he created an online dream forum. People would post a dream, share a brief snapshot of themselves and any significant events that might be taking place in their life, and then take a stab at what they thought their dream might mean. Then others in the forum would also work with the dream and post their insights.

Brugh insisted that dreams are sacred. It was his assertion that we are 99.99 percent unconscious, and in welcoming dreams and working with them, we can become more conscious, thus relying less on "fate" to guide our lives. During the retreat, I watched him work a lot with dreams fellow participants shared. While I liked what I saw and felt, I could not grok the language of dreams. It was an entirely new language—primarily a language of symbols. Because the symbols can have a uniquely personal meaning, a more tribal cultural meaning, or a more universal collective meaning, trying to discern between them was hard. It required a more intuitive touch; a literal interpretation of dreams and dream symbols rarely worked.

I read what folks were posting on the dream forum. Brugh and others would draw conclusions about the dreams that made no sense to me. I marveled at how utterly revealing dreams were and that it took courage to post unflattering and ego-deflating dreams. It seemed like no matter what anyone might try to hide about themselves, dreams would reveal all their secrets.

I missed the close intimacy and vulnerable sharing I had experienced at Brugh's retreat but could feel it again there in his online dream forum. I wanted to participate, but it would mean learning an entirely new language, and it would entail me trying to remember my dreams.

I started asking for a dream at bedtime. I would place a journal and a pen next to my bed, and following Brugh's instructions, I began requesting a dream nightly. Here was the process I was taught to request a dream:

> As I lie in bed, in my mind's eye, I picture myself standing at the edge of a high cliff. I remove all my clothing. I turn my back to the abyss. And, as I start to fall asleep, I fall backward into the abyss in total trust and then ask for a dream.

Night after night I do this, and I eventually start to have some dreams that I remember. I wake up and write them down faithfully. I post them online but can't fathom what they possibly mean. Still, I throw myself into the dream forum and into my dream world with as much energy and earnest sincerity as possible. The fearlessness in posting all manner of crazy and vulnerable dreams creates an intimacy between myself and others that I crave and that I am just beginning to learn and experience and appreciate.

And then the dreams began to gush forth. I went from not having or remembering any dreams to having and remembering three dreams a night—some nights it was five or six. I had to make an agreement with whoever or whatever was revealing all these dreams to me that, on some nights, I am allowed to just sleep and not be awakened by a dream or remember them. There were enthralling dreams of majesty and beauty as well as horrifying, frightening dreams. There were also some revealing and embarrassing dreams.

I wanted them all. The good and the bad. I wanted to be fearless and not hide anything about myself.

Some of my early dreams made sense even to me. Some hearkened back to when I was the store manager of several stores in a large regional grocery chain. When I began remembering and writing down my dreams, I would have dozens of dreams showing me that my store was growing, being remodeled, added on to, torn down, rebuilt, new departments added, etc. Weirdly, my bigger and better new store would often seem to be running itself!

Yep! If that store was me, that's how I experienced the journey—I began to grow and change and be remodeled and torn down and rebuilt and then expanded with lots of new departments, and periodically, I would also be emptied and then restocked with all new products, and along the way, I would be confused because it sometimes felt like I was in a sort of flow where things just happened on their own—even miraculous things—without "me" doing anything! I grew. I had more resources available to me. A sort of miraculous synchronistic flow of small and large miracles began to happen with greater and greater frequency.

Many years later, I realized the depth of information I gleaned from paying attention to my dreams. While there are many different types of dreams, overall, it felt like I, as I knew myself to be, was being taught *by* my dreams. They became my sort of go-to inner teacher and/or inner intuition, and as the dreams continued, I developed greater trust in them. And Brugh gave me another great gift: he taught me that by going to the heart center and approaching my dreams from there—a place of unconditional love and compassion—rather than from the mind or ego, I could sit with both the most terrifying and the most beatific dreams in a state of immense gratitude and appreciation. This was to serve me well as time went on, for I had no idea just how much unexpected awe-inspiring beauty and terrifying horror were to come.

3

Peeling Shrimp

I t is the summer of 2002, and I am just about to start group therapy. It is a circle composed primarily of women. I have never sat in a circle like this before. This is a new experience for me. I've never let myself open up to others and be vulnerable—especially to a bunch of women. I'm nervous.

Since I began my heart-centered meditation and began asking for dreams, I'm starting to have dreams, and the dreams seem to be helpful and trying to teach me and prepare me for things. On the night before one of my first group therapy meetings, I have a dream that seems to be a warning:

> *One of the women in my group is speaking to the entire group. "I'm worried about John because we are going to be peeling shrimp."*
>
> *At first, I nod in agreement and then say, "I love shrimp! Why is peeling shrimp a problem?"*
>
> *And the woman says, "Well, before you eat shrimp, first you gotta peel off the shells and peeling shrimp can be messy."*

It was. Painful. Hard. Scary. Messy. I spent an entire year guarding myself, and while I was happy to help remove the shells from others, I was not the slightest bit inclined to remove my own shell and expose my own tender flesh.

4

Try Being

I t is 2002. I am a divorced, single dad tucking my two kids, Eric and Kelsey, ages ten and twelve, into bed. I am rushing things like I always do—pj's on, brushing teeth, stuff ready for school the next day, read stories, and turn off the lights. Night after night, I rush through the same routine. I am good at it. My skills are in management, and I am great at strategy, planning, staying on task, and getting things done.

I tuck Kelsey in first and turn out her light. I go to Eric's bedroom next, and he is energized and happily babbling away about his day. I want him to be quiet so I can turn off the light and stay on schedule. But then I remember something.

I have been in group therapy for a few months now, and the members and the two therapists are always getting on me about "being." "John, you are so good at *doing*. Try *being*." Most of the group (as well as the two therapists) are women—mostly I am the only man in my group.

What the heck is *being*? I can't even conceptualize it. I'm a busy single dad, and I have a lot to do. I'm not sure this group is for me and if it will be of any use to me at all. *Being* isn't gonna fix my problems.

But while I am sitting on the edge of Eric's bed, I decide to give it a try. What did I have to lose? At least I could tell my group I gave it a shot. So, I just relax and really try to "be" while my son is babbling away. I'm not trying to rush him, shut him up, or worry about all the things I have on my to-do list. I just sit there, and I really listen.

I listen intently for a few minutes, and then suddenly, I am overwhelmed by what feels like a massive wave of love! Suddenly I am *so in love* with my son in a way I have never felt before. I *love* his excited babbling. I cannot believe what I am feeling now and how good it feels!

No one ever explained to me what might happen if I tried to just "be." I guess I just assumed it would somehow be sort of peaceful and maybe calming to my usual state of high anxiety and adrenaline. But this was love. *The* love. A love I had never ever felt before.

When Eric's babbling is complete, I give him a kiss good night.

I go to my bedroom in a happy and blissful state. I feel graced and blessed. Could it be that all those women in my therapy group know something I don't?

When I return to my therapy group, I am softer, more open, less critical, and humbler. Definitely humbler.

Many years have gone by since this night, and I don't experience the wave of love quite like that ever again. But I did learn to appreciate deep listening—something I am still learning and something I sometimes still forget to do. I am by nature more talkative, argumentative, and action oriented. But when I still myself and get out of my own way, I find that deep and sincere listening to others is a deeply peaceful state—blissful really—and in many ways far more preferable to talking.

Ever since that wave of love swept over me, I find that I love my son so deeply that I feel like I just light up every single time I am with him.

I love you, Eric!

5

An Intuitive Answer

It is the fall of 2002. I've just tucked my kids into bed, kissed them, and turned off their lights. I am getting into bed myself now, but I am sad and grieving for my son, Eric. It was his first day back at elementary school today, and it did not go well.

He was so excited to go back to school this morning—like can't-sleep, peeing-your-pants, and-jumping-up-and-down kind of excitement. But all the kids he wanted to hang with and play with at school were rejecting him. All my son's super-high back-to-school expectations were dashed on day one. He did sort of have a friend named Arta, and I asked him why he wasn't playing with him, and he said that Arta wasn't cool and that all the cool kids rejected him too.

My son is experiencing rejection on the first day of school, and it looks like the light has gone out of his eyes. It cuts me deeply. What parent isn't just a little upset when their kid is being rejected and cast out?

I have recently been introduced to Tarot, and I love all the images on the cards. I learned that Tarot can be used to get intuitive answers to difficult questions. I have been taught to use my intuition and let the images speak to me and my question rather than read the name of the card and the explanation in the book.

So, I pull out my Voyager Tarot deck and ask, "How can I help my son, Eric?"

I spend a minute with my hand on my heart center and enter a state of unconditional love. I feel like I am also in a state of selfless service. I spread out the cards, close my eyes, scan the cards with my hands, feel for just the right card, and then draw it and turn it over.

The card I draw looks to me like a pair of swans taking on the world. The intuitive hit is instantaneous. I immediately go back to my son's bedroom and ask him how it might feel to be best friends with Arta and to not worry about what the "cool" kids think. I suggest that maybe having one good best friend might be better than being friends with lots of cool kids.

The light returns to Eric's eyes. Yes! The excitement is back.

The next day, he zips out the door to school like it is the first day all over again. When he comes home, he is smiling. His new best friend is Arta, and Eric is glowing.

Eric and Arta are different. Eric's heritage is American, he lives in a divorced household with his dad (me) and sister, and we go out to eat a lot. Arta's heritage is Persian, and he lives with his mother, stepfather, brother, and grandma (who seemed to be cooking Persian food 24/7), and they tend to eat at home a lot. Eric is generous and focused on others; Arta is more independent and self-focused. Eric is not into school and academics; Arta is.

Following my experiment with Tarot, the boys stayed best friends all through school. They played on football and basketball teams together, formed some awesome heavy metal bands together, wrote all their own music, played in some big venues, traveled all over the United States, did paintball, airsoft, played video games, drove fast cars together, and remain good friends today.

Just now, I am looking at that card again, and I notice it says, "SYNERGY. SIX OF WORLDS," and the book that goes with the deck says the card is about teamwork and cooperation and achieving greater goals together than alone.

I had spent most of my life to that point relying on data and news and statistics and logic and the opinions of others and then spending hours musing and thinking, thinking, and thinking some more. But here was an answer to a challenging problem that seemingly came to me in an instant. So, from that day forward, I fall in love with intuition. I spend the rest of my life seeking intuitive answers to life's difficult questions.

6

Black and White

I have been in Brugh's dream forum for almost a year now, and I am starting to have more frequent dreams. I am disciplined about writing them down. Some seem to be of a teaching nature, designed to soften my very masculine, logical, and right or wrong view of the world. Here are some examples:

I see a child's top spinning on the floor. As it begins to slow, I see that the top is black and white. As it comes to a stop, I see black letters set on a white background that spell W-A-R.

I see what seems to be an X-ray view of my inner musculature, and it looks like a painful mass of tightly twisted black-and-white muscles.

I am in a large building with a solid glass front, fifty-foot ceilings, and white walls that feels like a modern university. There are thousands of people here, and they are all in a panic. There is a tiny black-and-white ball, like a marble with yin-yang symbols on it. It has been discovered that all who touch the yin-yang marble will die. Many have touched it. Even worse, all who have touched it are contagious, and all who come in contact with those who have touched it will also die.

Already, it is clear that the epidemic is out of control. Unfathomable numbers of people have spread the disease. It is everywhere. The word about the imminent death of all just came out now, and everyone is leaving the building. Some are angry, determined to kill the person who invented the black-and-white ball. Others are crazy with fear. Some stumble around like zombies. Everyone is leaving the building like a crazed tidal wave.

I am new to dreamwork and dream interpretation, but these dreams seem pretty clear-cut to me. Over the last year or two, it is starting to become clear to me that I am learning an entirely different way of living—a more whole, holistic, and feminine way—and it is new to me.

The first dream seemed to be pointing to my overly developed black-and-white thinking and that this leads to war. (No doubt that prior to this time in my life my preference was for black-and-white thinking, competition, and arguments.)

The second dream seemed to be pointing out how enmeshed and entwined this black-and-white thinking was in my physiology. Frankly, in the dream, it looked painful. Maybe it was teaching me that my black-and-white thinking could have a detrimental effect on my body, health, and overall happiness.

It took more time before I began to make sense of the last dream. Since the process I was in at that time felt more like a road to wholeness, I think this last dream spoke to the fear of my masculine ego when confronted with wholeness. It was like the male ego wanted nothing to do with balance or wholeness. To the ego, it felt like death.

There were more spiritual workshops, spiritual practices, yogic practices, psychological practices, etc. that were moving people toward wholeness than ever before. Integration was all the rage then—integrating masculine and feminine, soul and spirit, Heaven and

Earth, dark and light—and indeed an integration of all the arche-types and all the opposites is afoot. Even the medical field moves swiftly toward more holistic practices.

I spent a good portion of my life to this point engaged in argument, competition, logic, and black-and-white thinking. These dreams and many others yet to come would point toward a more holistic, more feminine approach to life. It was as if I were a student of an entirely new way of looking at and experiencing life.

7

Testing My Horoscope

I t is the fall of 2003. I read my horoscope almost daily. I don't take it seriously. It's just an amusing and entertaining habit. But this one was unusual. It said, "You will meet someone special. But they are out of your league so let them go."

It was more specific than usual, and for some reason, I decided to test it out.

I left work at lunchtime and had two errands to run. First stop was the pet store. I slowly walk the aisles of Denny's Pet World looking for this special person who was out of my league.

I feel really dumb looking closely at every woman in the store— both customers and employees alike. But today is a Tuesday, and there were hardly any customers in the store.

Then I go to Trader Joe's. I grab a grocery cart and slowly and purposely walk every aisle looking for my special someone.

Normally, when I shop or run errands, I am on a mission. I go in with a list, shop fast, and am in and out with shocking efficiency. This is different. I am walking slowly. I am looking everyone in the eyes. *Are you my special someone? Are you? You?*

Of course, I feel like a stalker too.

By the time I get to the last aisle, I am pretty sure this isn't going to happen. I have more food in my cart than I need, and I start the long, slow walk up to the checkout from the back of the last aisle.

Then I meet her.

Our eyes lock. She is my age—maybe a bit younger. She walks right up to me and starts casually chatting. She is commenting about all the food in my cart. I notice that she has a light cast on her lower leg. I ask about her leg. She is pretty and well put together. Nice clothes. Hair and nails all done to perfection. Nice figure. She looks lean and athletic.

Ummm . . . so what do I do now? Ask her out? I feel awkward.

I say goodbye and head for the checkout. *Should I have kept on talking? Asked for her phone number?*

She moves past me headed for the back of the store. I am up front and about to check out, and she looks like she is just about to start her shopping.

Dang. She was cute!

I get in line and am wondering what the hell I am doing here. I had not planned to *actually* meet someone and so I had no plan for what to do if it really happened.

As I get to the front of the line and the checker starts to ring up my groceries, the well-put-together mystery woman walks right back up to me and starts talking about the food I am buying again. She is friendly and talkative. It turns out she just needed one thing, and so now she is in line right behind me.

I have four bags of groceries in my cart and wheel them out to my car. *Should I ask her out?* I didn't see a ring on her finger. Do people meet in Trader Joe's and then ask for contact info? I don't know. I'm still a single dad and have not dated anyone yet since my divorce.

But as I place my last bag in the back of my minivan, I see her whisk out the door, give me a quick wave, jump into a sky-blue convertible Ford Thunderbird, and zip away.

Oh well. She was outta my league.

I think about this story often and wonder if on some level we are far more powerful than we know. That maybe we not only have the power to manifest our desires (if our intentions are clear), but that maybe we also have the power to influence how we see events. What if I'd gone into Trader Joe's and intended to find my soul mate for life, or maybe just a new friend and not someone "out of my league"?

What if we really *are* all connected to some vast and mostly invisible web and that, somehow, I sent out a radio signal saying, "I'm looking to meet someone who is out of my league," and my mystery woman picked up the signal and the request?

I had no interest in astrology at that time and knew nothing about it and read my horoscope just for fun, but it did occur to me that maybe all those folks who study the stars and planets might also have something to say about the unfolding of events in our lives.

Mostly, I just concluded that I need to be more conscious and aware of what I am thinking about most of the time. That maybe "be careful what you wish for" contains a lot of eternal wisdom, and that maybe all those folks who say we each "create our own reality" are correct.

8

Thine Eyes Becomes Single

I was having yet another argument with a man I know over politics. Again. It was a silly argument, but competitive arguing is a well-ingrained habit in me, and I am good at it. Later, I go home and take a quick nap and a dream springs forth . . .

I am fighting with the same man I was fighting and arguing with earlier in the morning. We both have big, red, puffy, and inflated heads like giant red balloons. Suddenly I see a giant eye in the sky above me. It grabs me by the seat of my pants and pulls me high into the sky. I am still arguing with the man below, and I see my big, red, inflated head and pumping fist—I just wanted to fight. I glance up and see that I am being drawn up into the giant eye. I disappear into the giant eye, and suddenly I feel so much peace. Silence. Endless Peace. A timeless infinite Peace.

I awoke and recalled the Bible quote from Matthew 6:22: "The light of the body is the eye: If therefore, thine eyes be single, thy whole body shall be full of light."

9

Blessings on the Special
Path of Fatherhood

I am out shopping for Christmas presents in early December 2003. Stonehouse is one of two or three local spiritual bookstores. I go in planning to see if I can purchase a few gifts and cross some names off my Christmas list all the while admonishing myself, "NO MORE BOOKS!" I have too many unread books already. I am here to buy gifts for others. No more books for me.

When I walk into the store, I am surprised to see that the author David Spangler has a special section of the store devoted to him and his books. I had just finished a small book by David entitled *The Call* that was meaningful to me. I didn't know he had written so many other books, nor did I know that he was quite popular.

I peruse the books and ignore the "NO MORE BOOKS" voice in my head. One of David's books practically jumps into my arms. It is titled *Parent as Mystic, Mystic as Parent*. I'm doing my best to raise my two children on my own while starting to have a bunch of mystical experiences. I don't have any other moms and dads to share such experiences with, and I sometimes feel lonely. I skim the book, and I see that the entire book is about raising kids (David has four kids) while being a mystic. I feel such a relief and an affinity for both the author and the book.

I grab the book and one other. I never do find any Christmas gifts and head for the cashier.

The cashier is warm and friendly and has read the books I am purchasing and shares her positive reviews of both. Then she says, "Would you like to meet him?"

"Who?" I ask.

"David. The author."

I turn around, and at that precise moment, a short, grandfatherly-looking man emerges from a room in the back with dozens of folks milling about him. The cashier calls to David to come and meet me and to sign my books.

David walks up to me, and I stammer a bit, caught off guard. I recall that Dr. William Brugh Joy had written the foreword to David's book *The Call,* so I mention that I have worked with Brugh as a conversation starter.

David warmly greets me and asks about Brugh. "How is Brugh doing these days?"

"Fine," I tell him and share that I recently spent ten days with him in one of his conferences out in the desert.

David informs me that he and Brugh used to regularly work together and did an annual New Year's Day gathering in Asilomar on the Monterey Peninsula in California. Then he sees the books I am purchasing and asks about my kids. We laugh and share some stories about raising kids.

It turns out that David is sort of famous. He was one of the founders of the Findhorn community in Scotland and was one of the young leaders of the New Age movement. It also turns out that he lives close by. Our homes are just twenty minutes apart! I had no idea!

I feel a comfort in his presence and the message he offers to me is that one can be a mystic *and* a parent at the same time. It's a bit unusual, but being a mystic enriches parenting and does not distract from it.

David grew up having mystical experiences. I did not. Mine are new to me. I'd lived a rigid, rational, and competitive view of life for decades, and now I sometimes didn't know what to do with the mystical experiences. I sometimes feel elated. Sometimes lonely. Sometimes scared. Sometimes my old rigid personality wanted to just explain them all away as nothing more than worthless fantasy.

Again, David is warm, and I appreciate his grounded, self-deprecating humor. What parent hasn't been humbled by the experience of raising children on more than one occasion? While I am doing my best as a single father, it's still sometimes hard. I appreciate just being in David's presence.

David takes my book and signs it: "To John. With blessings on the special path of fatherhood."

I take the book home and read it from cover to cover and it feels like a balm to all of my anxieties and fears. Mystical experiences? Raising kids? Sure! I embrace them both with enormous gratitude.

Thank you, David!

10

Revitalizing Bernie

It is early 2004, and I am attending my second-ever spiritual workshop. Dr. William Brugh Joy is leading the weekend, and there are about thirty of us in a home owned by a doctor in the upscale community of Medina, Washington. Though I met Brugh about eighteen months earlier at his "Foundational Conference"—a spiritual retreat out in the desert in Southern California—I am still really new to spiritual work. I haven't had many spiritual experiences up to this point, but I do like the deep sharing with others and working with my dreams.

We spend the first day and a half meditating and mostly working with dreams.

In the afternoon of the second full day, Brugh announces that we are now going to do some healing work. He introduces us to an elderly man in a wheelchair. Bernie has a terminal illness of some kind and apparently traditional Western medicine has nothing more to offer him. Frankly, he looks ill, quite frail, and his skin has the same sort of pallor heavy smokers have.

It is Brugh's diagnosis that Bernie had long since lost touch with his body. Bernie was a brilliant academic who had done amazing work at Stanford University. Brugh suggested we look him up when we got a chance so that we could see all of Bernie's achievements.

Brugh announces that this afternoon's healing work is going to be about trying to restore Bernie's awareness of and appreciation for his body. He then asks for very specific volunteers: People who highly identify with both their mind and their body, who are at home using their mind but also have a strong connection to and appreciation for their physicality.

Hmmm. Well, that sounds like me. I am always in my head and always reading lots of books, and I consider myself intelligent. But I also love my physicality—I do triathlons and enjoy swimming, surfing, mountain biking—heck, just about any physical activity!

I cautiously raise my hand, certain I will not be chosen because I've never done any healing work. But Brugh looks at me, appraises me, and then slowly says, "Yes."

As it turns out, there are about six of us who fit the description Brugh is looking for. He then asks us to surround Bernie in a sort of group hug, and as he plays some quiet music, he asks us to get in touch with the part of us that loves our body and our physicality and then to send that love of our physicality and our body to Bernie.

As Brugh starts the music, I am working hard to find that part of me and send it to Bernie. But I am also extremely self-conscious. I've never done healing work, and I am standing in a circle surrounded by dozens of other people. *What the heck am I doing here?*

For what feels like five full minutes, nothing happens. I am trying to send my love of physicality to Bernie while simultaneously feeling like a fraud and a fake and just wanting to get this all over with.

And then . . .

In an instant, it is like a switch is flipped, and I am swept up in an energy that is so palpable, so electric, and so enlivening that words can't capture it. In that same moment, in my mind's eye, I see myself as one of those cliff divers in Mexico leaping off a one-hundred-foot-high cliff in an ecstatically perfect joy-filled swan dive. Our entire little group of volunteers is swept up in this energy, and for the next fifteen minutes, we are all swimming in a sea of ecstatic joy. We are no longer sending anything to Bernie—there is just this ball of ecstatic joy! We are all literally vibrating in ecstasy, and I can so *feel* my love of my body and physicality, and I am joyfully sharing this with Bernie!

After about twenty minutes it ends, and I have to crawl off in a corner and be alone. My entire body is reeling from too much pleasure. I had zero idea that anything like this was even possible. I am so caught up in my ecstatic pleasure that I forget to even ask Bernie what the experience was like for him, nor did I know if it had helped.

Two years later, Brugh came to the Puget Sound area again and was hosted by a woman in Olympia, and I decided to attend. And there, on the first day, was Bernie! He still looked sort of old and frail but had a sparkle in his eyes and was looking dapper in a green Nike tracksuit and running shoes. I overheard him talking about what a great personal trainer he had. It made me smile.

How often do you get the opportunity to share a part of yourself that you really love and truly offer it to another in such a profound and unexpected way?

Years later I bumped into one of the women who was part of the group that surrounded Bernie with me. She was living in Seattle. She told me it was one of the top-ten experiences of her life. Mine too.

11

Healing the Pain in My Neck

It is early 2004, and I have come home from work early. I am in tears.

I have had neck pain for approximately the last six years. I was rear-ended in a car crash, and being a tough guy, I never went to the doctor. Over time, I developed chronic whiplash-type neck pain.

Most days I would wake up in the morning and my neck would not be in much pain, but it seemed like everything I did in the course of my day made it hurt. Driving to work hurt it. Sitting in front of my PC hurt it. Stress hurt it. Sitting on a couch watching TV hurt it. Standing still hurt it.

I tried everything to make it better: pillows behind my back when sitting, standing in front of my PC, sitting on a bouncy ball at work, stretching, and relaxing. I got books on neck pain and followed all the exercises faithfully. I did physical therapy. Ultrasound. Massage. Acupuncture. Chiropractic. Everything seemed to help a bit, but only briefly.

I even went so far as to have surgery—a last resort—where they put me under and injected cortisone between the facet joints in my neck. But the only relief I felt was when they gave me the anesthetic. When I woke up and the anesthetic wore off, the pain was back.

So here I am now, home from work early and in tears. I can't believe I will have to live like this for the rest of my life. I am only in my forties, and I love being active and athletic.

I crawl in bed and mumble to myself, "Why the fuck does my neck hurt so badly?"

Almost instantly I fall asleep and just as fast have a dream . . .

I see a monk with a shaved head in red robes walking outside my house. He is pacing back and forth at the end of my driveway.

Somehow that dream seemed to be trying to answer my question, but I could not grasp how this monk pacing back and forth in front of my house in a dream had anything to do with my neck pain. I posted my dream on Brugh's dream forum, which I had recently joined, with the history about my neck pain and how the dream seemed to be in response to it.

Brugh jumped in and simply said, "That dream has EVERYTHING to do with your neck pain."

He didn't explain and I didn't get it, so I asked for more help. Brugh asked me to explore what the color red symbolizes. Why do monks wear robes? Why do they shave their heads? Why might a monk be pacing back and forth in front of my house (instead of, say, someone else's house)? Why is the monk *outside* my house (rather than, say, *inside* my house)?

Over time, Brugh helped me to see from the dream that I had a spiritual side, and I was still in complete denial of this, and thus this side of me, this selfless monk, was not welcome in my "house."

This was probably true. I had been sort of selfish, competitive, and overly rational for many years and had spent decades pushing all things and all people that I deemed religious or spiritual as far away as possible.

Brugh asked me to open up to the possibility that the dream was showing me I had another "self" who was a monk and that even if this monk seemed foreign to my own current or past sense of self to see if I might let him in and allow my self-identity to change and evolve.

So, I tried. It did not happen overnight. I really tried to open and see a spiritual and more selfless monk side of me. Sometime after that, I had another dream . . .

I see Brugh coming toward me to heal my neck pain. I am so thankful. Finally! But as he reaches for my neck, an angry old man who lives in my neck gruffly yells, "Get the fuck away!"

So, no healing. And, apparently, I also had an angry old man living in my neck.

But I kept opening to this monk as a part of me.

Maybe two years later, I had another dream . . .

I am sitting in my home office and am holding a giant golden thumbtack. I absentmindedly reach over and push the tack into the wall behind me, but it feels weird. I look behind me to see why it felt so weird, and there in my house, I see a monk with shaved head in red robes standing over me, the golden thumbtack piercing his heart and him smiling broadly at me with such love.

It has been about two years since the first monk dream, and my neck pain is GONE. Yes, really gone. Not in one instant. It was more like I woke up one day and realized it just wasn't there anymore.

What Brugh taught me with that experience was simply that I held resistance in my neck. Anything I was fighting or resisting or defending against would end up as a stiff neck or neck pain. But the dream made what I was fighting against conscious, and it revealed what was really going on deep inside me.

I can still feel the absolute despair I was in—the constant tears and anger over what I feared would be a lifetime of endless chronic pain with no cure. But, in the end, there *was* a cure. I would never have guessed though that the cure would have come about through inviting a monk into my home!

12

A Night in Philadelphia

It's August 2004. I'm in a hotel in Philadelphia, trying to go to sleep. I have to get up at 5:00 a.m. to return home to Seattle. But I'm too happy to sleep. Earlier that evening I had appeared live on QVC—the home-shopping network. It was the first time I had ever appeared live on national TV.

I own a consumer products company, and we make a whole line of biodegradable and nontoxic branded cleaning and pet products sold in thousands of retail stores across the country. This was a big opportunity to promote our products on live TV nationwide. I was feeling some pressure as the QVC folks said I would have about 700,000 new viewers per minute. Yikes!

But I survived my seven minutes of fame and didn't embarrass myself on live national TV. Plus, I sold a fair amount of product.

Back at my hotel, my body is buzzing with joy—so much so that I'm wide awake. I assume all the joy is simply the relief that my live appearance on TV is behind me now and that I didn't screw up. Or maybe I'm wide awake because of the three-hour time difference; I'd just flown in from Seattle the night before, and I had not yet adjusted to East Coast time.

I do a light meditation to try to relax. In the meditation, I see what looks like light plunging down from above deep into my body and then back up again—like a plunger of light going up and down.

But still . . . I can't sleep. I am feeling so happy, so joyous, so energized.

At around midnight, I am still awake but sort of happily dozing when I am suddenly and unexpectedly overwhelmed by what feels like an orgasmic wave that runs through the core of my body from my perineum up and out through the top of my head. It lasts a few seconds and feels like an uncontrollable but pleasurable fire. My legs and arms seem to catch the excess energy, and they feel overwhelmed with tingly adrenaline.

This repeats over and over again. It feels completely out of my volitional control. It is erratic and unpredictable, and I never know which wave is going to be the last. It feels sexual. Primal. Powerful.

Repeated slow-motion explosions of powerful waves of joy are surging from below to above. I surrender willingly—but not without the background thoughts of fear. Whatever was happening to me—however joyful it felt—also seemed to freak out the Catholic boy in me who was in fear. It felt like something "out there" was entering me and, being so unknown (I had no idea anything like this was even possible), it was really disconcerting.

But some other part of me was riding the waves of immense joy and well-being and in total trust. Imagine wave after wave of powerful, hot orgasmic bliss surging upward in slow motion. It's not the kind of thing one simply tells to go away!

At maybe 3:00 a.m. or so, I decide I've had enough. My logical mind kicks in to say that it is three in the morning, and I still have not slept. I walk back and forth in my room trying to shake off all the joyful energy. I return to bed and sleep for maybe an hour or two and then get up and head for the airport.

On the flight home, I am both very tired and highly energized. I have this inner sense that whatever happened to me was some sort of grace or miracle, but still there is the fear around the unknown.

Upon return, I contact some folks I had met in Brugh's conference and retreat and described my experience and asked them if they knew what it was. "Kundalini rising" seemed to be the consensus, and they suggested I look it up. I'd heard of the term but had no idea what it actually was.

I even wrote Brugh himself and he simply said, "Be patient with this development" and wisely did not make a big deal out of it. I was relieved that everyone agreed it was normal (even if a bit uncommon) and that all cultures around the globe spoke of this energy and that each had their own name for it. I looked it up and bought some books. The description of energy rising from the root chakra (perineum area) up through the central channel along the spine and arriving at the crown chakra (the top of the head) matched my experience. And the description of the energy itself as earth energy, feminine energy, sexual energy, hot and fiery energy, and powerful, primal energy all matched my experience as well.

This all gave me an even greater sense of peace, safety, and relief. This had happened to many others throughout the world. Books had been written on it. It was actually something others sought and desired. Suddenly a memory popped into my head. About a week before the onset of the Kundalini energy, I'd had a hyper-vivid dream:

> It is a hot August afternoon. The sun is low on the horizon. I am lying naked in the arms of Mother Nature herself in a meadow full of wildflowers gently swaying in the dry, late-afternoon breeze. She is reaching down between my legs—as if she were somehow loosening a screw and opening something in my perineum.

This felt like another precognitive dream. Looking back, it seemed to be announcing that something was being opened in me. If what was happening to me was indeed earthy, sexual, primal, feminine energy, who better than Mother Nature herself to initiate the process?

13

Immersion into the Goddess

Without knowing it at the time, I was being initiated into the Goddess and indeed into all things feminine. My therapy group was mostly composed of women who were always pushing me into areas I struggled with: listening deeply, asking for help, being instead of doing, intuiting instead of just thinking rationally, allowing instead of pushing, allowing feelings—all of them—and actually feeling them and expressing them with fearless honesty, revealing myself fully, and being vulnerable.

Even Brugh was pushing me in that direction: "Just try it, John. You won't lose your wonderful and highly developed masculine. You will be more whole and more resourceful."

Come to think of it, since my divorce and having custody of my kids, nearly all of my friends were women. I was hanging out with all the other single moms—I was becoming one of them! And unbeknownst to me, the Kundalini energy was taking the new feminine journey I was on to a whole new level.

Another recent dream popped into my consciousness, seeming to confirm my further initiation into all things feminine:

I am back in my old job as a grocery store manager in a large regional chain. I'm nervous because I've been away for a long time and might not know how things are done now. Even worse, the entire store is being run by women who happily and excitedly tell me not to worry—that they will train me and teach me everything. I look down at my keys and see that instead of the large wad of keys I used to have, my key ring now has only five golden keys on it. Attached to the key ring is also a golden rune, and on the rune, it says, "Student Discount 1999–2012."

Two nights after my initial onslaught of Kundalini energy in Philadelphia, the energy returns. I'm in bed alone and at about 1:00 a.m., it comes again. Exactly as before, the long, slow, blissful waves of power move upward from my root chakra to my crown chakra. Over and over.

But there is one difference. I am in my bed lying on my back with my legs and arms both spread wide. Now I feel energy entering the palm of one hand and traveling across my chest and out the palm of my other hand. Imagine tiny tissues entering your palm and being dragged across and through your chest and out the other palm. Back and forth it goes—over and over—like I am being cleaned out with delicate cloths.

I wake up feeling giddy, tired, and twitchy, like I am high on a pleasant drug and had too much caffeine.

I spend some time online seeing if I can find instances of Kundalini entering one's palm, traveling across the chest, and exiting the other palm but cannot. So again, it feels like something "out there" has entered me and the fear arose again.

I feel both gratitude, grace, fear, and humility. It's hard not to feel at least a little bit humble when things are happening beyond volitional control and/or beyond comprehension. I LIKE being in CONTROL. I like PLANS and STRATEGY and ORDER!

A couple nights later, it all happens again but only briefly—a couple of mild waves and one immense one. But then, on the night of Sunday, August 8, 2004, at 3:26 a.m., I am cracked wide open. I furiously take notes to try to capture it all:

- *Kundalini takes me on a ride through time, pattern, space, texture, light, and liquid. Beauty and power in 3D like nothing I have ever seen. It is the night of 1,000 paintings all in such majesty. Hour upon hour of explosions in my root, quivering twitches in my entire body.*
- *Visions of ancient sages all in hyper vivid 3D—very old and very powerful. I see an old Asian man with a single lens covering his eye in the middle of his forehead; there are glittering rainbow diamonds in 3D set against the gorgeous black night sky. There are textures, fabrics, and liquid pouring and manifesting and materializing into things of incredible beauty.*
- *Your life will never be the same.*
- *I am sharing the Creator working through me. I see an art gallery of:*
  - LIGHT: Light that melts hard hearts and makes them cry tears of joy.
  - DIMENSIONS: No end, no beginning, no left or right, top or bottom, right or wrong. Infinite.
  - DIAMONDS: Made of rainbows and set in black infinite space in great 3D depth. Reflecting all that is inside and containing the full spectrum of light.
  - WATER: Life pouring forth and manifesting into an infinite number of life forms.
  - TEXTURES, FABRICS, PATTERNS: The Love of the Universe. We are all woven together.
  - ANCIENT SAGES: Wizened, gray. Carrying a burden of the secrets of existence.
  - ONE-EYED ASIAN MAN: Single-focused devotion.
  - DARKNESS: The light looks so glorious next to it!
  - ELECTRICITY: Movement and change.
  - AURA: Love. People's auras can have hooks, and hook into each other.

- WOMEN: Creativity and community.
- *Lie still. The images surge with energy and life. Electric! The body and mind allow for seeing and feeling the images. What a gift!*
- *Clouds appear in early morning—a rapid-fire staccato of a thousand shades of dawn. Tears of awe and appreciation.*
- *I lay my head in the arms of Mother Nature. She has appeared and I trust her. Which is good because my life will never be the same.*
- *Thank you, God, for my being alive. Help me to trust you and to love life. To be happy and just trust. To feel that giddy sense of life again.*
- *Go slow. Be patient with me. My fabric is stained, my crown is old, and my mask is crumbling. I am on my knees. What grace.*

For the next couple of months, the onslaught of energy continues. It seems to come every two or three nights, and I'm always in a state of gratitude and joy upon its return. I still struggle the mornings after the energy shows up because the joy and energy are so intense that it wrecks my sleep. So, I slog through my day—both exhausted and yet feeling graced. But interspersed are great waves of fear too.

Day after day it goes like this—the energy comes at night, and generally I am in a state of awestruck joy. I cannot believe what is happening to me. I wake up exhausted and struggle to get through my day. Fear starts to enter my mind and preys on it throughout the day. I go to bed and sleep deeply with no dreams and no energetics. The next day is much better—I have more energy and feel more positive, yet I begin to miss the energy. Then it comes again, and the cycle is repeated. It seems very wise; it knows when to push me and when to pull back.

I make the mistake of talking about it with my mother, who, while very wedded to a strict Catholic path, has had some mystical experiences of her own, so I thought she might have something to offer. But the conversation quickly turns to Satan and demons and then later I read some stuff online where Christians are saying Kundalini is demonic possession. I acknowledge that I truly don't know what it is and that, at times, I am in a state of trepidation and great fear.

In the midst of all my fear, the energy seems to up and leave. Now I feel angry that my mother and Catholics and Christians have stolen something precious from me. An entire week goes by with no energy but lots and lots of dreams, and I trust the dreams. They seem to say that I am OK—just going through a very deep transformation into all things feminine.

If I were to summarize all the dreams during this period of my life it might look like this:

I am in the belly of the Queen Mary sinking deep into the ocean. My grocery store is run by women. I have dozens of women in my dreams and have sex with nearly all of them. There are dark-black women, fiery red-haired women, earthy women with long lush hair, young sexy women, old ancient women, Asian women, a woman who says I will marry her sister, "Unison." I even meet the Goddess Kundalini, and she appears to me as a jet-black naked woman, maybe two-feet tall, and she is strong, lean, athletic, and working feverishly on some part of my body.

One of the ways this seemed to manifest in my waking life, which was quite strange, was that the energy and all the sex with all manner of goddesses at night had created a sexual fury in me that was overwhelming. I was sex crazed! And yet the energy was so intense that I felt spent the next day. I was desperate for sex but too exhausted to actually have sex with a real, live woman!

Many years later, I met a woman in the throes of this energy, and she had created a business where she was doing sex therapy with paying clients—imagine a woman with almost infinite sexual desire who was both sexually serving clients and spiritually teaching at the same time. When we met and I told her my own story, she was so overjoyed to be so seen by another. I totally understood her almost insatiable desire!

A few years later I read the autobiography of Swami Muktananda wherein he too went through a Kundalini phase of epic sexual desire, and he was an avowed celibate! Every single day he would close his eyes and see a fiery goddess framed in fire who would sexually arouse him and cause him great embarrassment.

I begin to trust that all of this is by design and not something to be afraid of. There seems to be a wide variety of perceptions of Kundalini—everything from something to be feared and rejected to something to be revered and grateful for. I read more books on Kundalini, and some of the stories frighten me. I have obligations and responsibilities as a single dad and business owner, so I am fearful of somehow being so altered that I cannot function. And there is the fear of the energy itself—some of the stories I read are quite harrowing! In some cases, there was great pain, and the Kundalini fire did indeed sometimes feel like a blowtorch!

But even with all that, I am in love with it. Every single night I simply cannot wait to tuck my kids in, climb in bed myself, and wait to see what might happen.

While I never did have another night like the night of Sunday, August 8, 2004, for a few years after the initial onset, I did have repeated energetic experiences that would come roughly every second or third night that in summary mostly looked like this:

- Light to moderate waves in the root/perineum area with some of them moving up to the crown.
- Powerful waves in my root/perineum and visions of "Golden Dust" (greenish globules with glowing yellow cores floating all around me)
- A long series of pleasant electric shocks
- Great force lasting for hours
- Twitchy shocks
- Long and powerful and so joyful—like on an endless joyous ride
- Rapid fire staccato powerful shocks and waves

- Explosions in my root chakra
- Obsession with sex

Sometimes the energy would do really strange things—like one time it entered my kneecap with great force! And even though I seemed to be asleep when all the energetics occurred, the energy would usually wake me up, and I would just lie there and allow it to happen—usually in a state of awe and gratitude and sometimes great fear and apprehension.

Weirdly, my body was in full participation; I sometimes found myself waking up in strange yoga positions, such as with the soles of my feet pressed together and both feet pulled up to my perineum—and I didn't do yoga! In many cases, I would awaken with both hands placed over my heart center, and in some cases, my hands seemed to be moving with the energy as if I was helping to draw the energy upward from root to crown by tracing the path with my hands.

During this period, I was continually blasted by energy from outside me as well. I had dreams where I was walking around my house and would walk into a room—say the kitchen—and just get mauled and crushed by energy of enormous force that would always wake me up.

In these dreams it was, I imagine, like being in an electric chair, and it would send me to my knees grimacing in pain. I just endured it. Over and over these dreams came, and the veil between dream and waking was very thin. I would come out of the dreams exhausted and spent, feeling like I had barely survived a painful and crushing ordeal. Other times I would have dreams that I was walking along the ocean and lightning would erupt from out of the ocean and zap my body and the palms of my hands. One evening, I was lying awake in bed, dozing a bit, and I could see a swirling, twisted mass of bluish-white light (like a giant living ball of yarn made of light) hovering above me, and then suddenly, a bolt of lightning from this "source" blasted my heart center, as if it were zapped with heart paddles for cardiac arrest.

It takes time, but I start to find a way to settle into a routine with work and with my kids that accommodate all the strange experiences

I am having and all the lost sleep. The school bus drops my kids off at home just after 4:00 p.m. I start coming home early from work to try to squeeze in a nap just before they get home. I fall into a habit where I barely put my head on the pillow for these late-afternoon mini naps, and I am instantly in a dream—except the dreams are SO REAL! As was so often the case before, the dreams are full of goddesses. One afternoon I have a dream . . .

> *I am being spooned from behind by a gorgeous naked goddess. Her graceful arms reach around my body from behind me, and I see what looks like a radio dial in my belly. Her long and slender fingers are adjusting the dial—trying to find a particular and very subtle station. When she finds it, my entire body explodes in bliss! I shift my body a bit, and she loses the station and has to seek it again. Over and over, we play this game of "find the very subtle station and explode in bliss and then lose it and then begin the search for it again."*

The next day, I again almost instantly fall into a nap and again a gorgeous, naked goddess appears in my dream:

> *A beautiful goddess is sitting on my tailbone, and I am pinned down. She is searching for just the right spot in my perineum area. She finds it, and somehow, she blows a mighty wind throughout my entire body! I can see and feel a wind blowing through my body and out every single pore. Every single hair on my body is flapping at high speed as this mighty wind exits my body.*

It is one thing to have a dream wrapped in the arms of a luscious, sexy, naked goddess in which she tries to fill my body with great bliss, but it is quite another where I feel powerless to move as she blows a powerful wind through my entire body—that felt like terror! Still, I had this sense, even being pinned down and having a wind blown through my body, that this was perhaps some sort of purification, so I learned to just roll with it—sort of like an instant spiritual cleanse!

Seemingly every single late-afternoon nap included a goddess visitation. There were magnificent goddesses with white hair in long braids wrapped up on top of their heads with entirely white eyes (no iris or pupils), looking very much like regal queens. There were also mysterious goddesses with eyes that were entirely black.

Some of the dream experiences were downright scary. For instance:

I am cuddling a small woman—almost the size of a baby—with great love. She is snuggled up in a ball next to my chest sound asleep. I am looking at her with such love, and she seems to be very happy here. I move my body a bit, which wakes her up. She looks up at me not expecting me to be awake, and she suddenly rears back and hisses at me like a wildcat with sharp teeth right in my face, and I see her gold eyes have cat-like pupils. She swiftly flies away.

These dreams and visitations felt incredibly real—like I was asleep and awake at the same time. And yet, every weekday, at around 4:00 p.m., the school bus would drive up, the kids would jump off, run to the front door, and ring the doorbell, and my wondrous and terrifying encounters with all manner of goddesses would evaporate. I was a dad then, attending to my kids, asking about their day and what homework they had, and making after-school snacks while getting ready to head out to sports team practices or other after-school activities.

14

The Shed

I t is 2004, and I am having a dream . . .

*I walk around back to a small garden shed at my parents'
house, and I hear a voice I recognize. It sounds like a gal friend
of mine named Kim, who is of Native American ancestry. Kim
emerges from the shed, and I am shocked to see that she is
half her normal weight and sickly white—like she hasn't been
outdoors in a very long time. Her hair is short and bleached,
though normally her hair is black, and her skin is dark. She is
naked, and her body is covered with blood-red splotches that
look like old scars or scabs. Her skin is rough and stiff as if it
were burned in a fire. I go and just hold her for a long time.
Our cheeks are tenderly touching. She smiles and laughs and
says something to me about her condition and blames it on
something, the name of which I don't quite catch.*

During this period, I was attempting to embrace all things and all
aspects of human life most people would attribute to women and/or
the feminine. I was learning to listen better. I was learning to be more

caring and more compassionate. I was learning to be more nurturing and more open to community and support. I hung out with single moms. I practiced being both Dad and Mom with my kids. I was more patient and more open to just allowing things. I was more open to feelings and things like intuition. I was less competitive.

My dream of Kim seemed to symbolize that I was somehow freeing my inner feminine and indeed maybe my entire family's lineage of sort of ignoring and/or imprisoning the feminine. I took the dream as a good sign.

15

Behind Appearances

I t's late 2004, and I'm taking my twelve-year-old daughter, Kelsey, and her two girlfriends out to eat at a local Chinese restaurant. Our waitress is Chinese, unusually tall, and slender. She takes our order and walks back into the kitchen through a metal swinging door.

The girls are happily babbling away. The restaurant is moderately crowded. I watch our waitress wait on other tables. She is tall, slope shouldered, and bucktoothed. Pretty unattractive. She has no butt and no boobs. My male judge is in full force.

She walks back into the kitchen area through the swinging metal door. Then about a minute later she walks back out and looks directly at me, and it is as if all time stands still. Suddenly, she is the loveliest woman in the world. Her face is now breathtakingly beautiful. The entire scene looks like one of those old black-and-white movie romances where the frame around the scene is fuzzy and diffuse. Every judgment I ever had melts in the presence of this extraordinary beauty. It is Beauty incarnate in a field of immense love.

And, in maybe five or ten seconds, it ends. The girls are still babbling away. The other patrons are still chattering, and if anyone else
saw what I just saw, they make no note of it.

I look around. Nothing.

Even the waitress seems oblivious.

This is a new experience for me. I don't have a wild imagination.
I'm not clairvoyant. I don't "see things" when I am awake. But, in that
fleeting moment, I *did* see something. Someone else. Something else.
Her soul? Her essence? *The* Goddess?

I have looked for that extraordinary beauty that seems to tran-
scend mere appearances in others many times. Looking. Peering.
Waiting. Hoping. But nothing quite like this happens ever again. But
ever since that evening, I do my best to never judge someone solely
on their outer appearance ever again.

16

A Message for Tammy

Around the time all the Kundalini energetics began in me in late 2004, I met a woman on Brugh's dream forum named Tammy, and I had become enamored with her. I'd never met anyone as psychic and intuitive as she. She lived in Chicago and I in Seattle, so we spent all our time on the phone and exchanging long emails.

I was intrigued by all things psychic and intuitive and was awestruck that she seemed to be able to read my every thought. I barely knew her, and yet it felt like we had been married for fifty years. She was the first person I'd ever met who seemed so unusually gifted psychically but who wasn't weird in any way—she had a grounded Midwestern sensibility, which helped me to trust her. The conversations I had with Tammy were deep and meaningful.

Over time, Tammy made it clear that she wanted us to have a date—a long weekend together. I was attracted to her, and the sexual energy I was experiencing with the Kundalini energy was overwhelming me. So, we made a date—I flew out to Chicago to spend a three-day weekend with Tammy.

We meet at the airport, go straight to our hotel room, and take our clothes off. I feel sex crazed, but at the same time, my sexual energy seems to have been zapped by all the energetics in my body that I keep experiencing at night. My body does not quite keep up with my desire.

Still, for a man in his mid-forties, the sex is frequent. We have sex almost continuously, interspersed with long, deep, meaningful conversations and meals out at restaurants.

Now it is our last full day together. Tammy is telling me that she has been a massage therapist for twenty years. She is also telling me that, over time, she began to get messages from people's bodies and that in the course of her massage therapy practice she began sharing these messages with her clients. As time went on, people started coming to her more for the messages than for the massage.

Again, very much intrigued as I am now with psychic things like "messages from the body," I ask her how she does it.

She says, "It's easy. Hold my feet. The feet are a great place to get messages."

So I hold her bare feet. I press them to my chest and wait for messages.

Nothing is happening. I am holding the feet of a woman I have only just met in person, hoping to get psychic messages from her body.

Nothing is happening.

I try harder.

Nothing.

My head is full of voices: *You are trying too hard—just relax. She has been doing this for TWENTY YEARS—you are not going to get any messages on your first try. You suck at this.*

I try to quiet the voices and concentrate harder. That doesn't work, so I try harder to let go and relax. Still nothing happens. Now I feel embarrassed. I feel like an idiot sitting here holding the feet of this virtual stranger, trying to get messages from her body.

But after maybe the longest three minutes of my life, I suddenly get this crystal-clear vision in my mind's eye of a young girl, maybe three or four years old, in white underpants, looking back over her shoulder and running away in abject terror. She is surrounded by near-total darkness.

I was expecting a voice, not a vision. I thought maybe her body would actually talk to me. But something deep inside me wanted me to do something with the vision.

My grounded Midwestern woman with psychic gifts looks at me expectantly. I don't tell her what I saw, but I ask her if I can do what is coming to me spontaneously.

"Yes, but I might cry," she says.

Something is about to happen, and weirdly, I think she knows it.

She lies on her back, and I sit next to her. I place my right hand over my heart chakra and my left hand on her heart chakra. And, instantaneously, what feels like two sharp jolts of energy, literally like two bolts of lightning, enter my body at my right shoulder and shoot down across my body and down my left arm into her heart center like . . . BOOM! BOOM! And then, in that moment, I am but a witness. Some Christ-like aspect has entered and found the terrified little girl of my vision and is surrounding the little girl in a coat of white light and is telling her that she never has to be afraid ever again. The little girl is clutching her new coat of white light in great joy with a huge smile on her face, and her coat of white light is so bright that it lights up everything around her—crowding out all the darkness.

In maybe ten seconds it is over.

My date is sobbing.

I did nothing but offer and open and then just watch.

I feel graced beyond belief. Nothing like this has ever happened to me. I had no idea anything like this was even remotely possible. And yet I also feel uncomfortable. I was not "trained" for this. What do I do now?

Later we go to dinner and my date shares with me that, when she was four years old, her father walked out on her family and just up and disappeared. And it seems that, in that moment, a terrified and abandoned little four-year-old girl just never grew up. My psychic, yet grounded, Midwestern date was in her forties, but the fearful four-year-old girl still lived on inside her.

Until today. The four-year-old girl who lived on inside her was still there, but apparently, she was no longer living in abject terror and darkness.

As for Tammy, we never dated again. She wanted to. I was afraid. I was still mildly freaked out by what had transpired. I was still a single dad, and the experience was so overwhelming that I needed time to make sense of it all. I just wanted to go back to work and back to being a dad.

A year later, Tammy met the man of her dreams and got married for the first time. She said that she was very happy with her husband. I have not heard from her in over ten years. As time has gone on, I continue to marvel at what I loosely call *healing*. What had her life been like with a terrified, abandoned child living inside her? And what was her life like now that the little girl was no longer fearful and frightened?

And what of the healer? Why did this light energy need to pass through a body (in this case mine) before entering the body of another? Was there a precise plan or destiny involved? Was it predetermined that Tammy would live with this frightened little girl inside her, and then one day, when she was in her forties, some bumbling innocent would hold her feet, hoping to get psychic messages but instead get a vision, then have light pass through him into her so the little girl would no longer be afraid, and then the woman would get happily married? It is all an awe-inspiring mystery.

More than a decade later, I still feel a connection to that four-year-old girl and to the psychic, grounded Midwestern woman. I feel gratitude for the experience and for our short time together, and I hope they are well.

17

Enter the Void

I am having a dream . . .

A booming voice says, "ENTER THE VOID!"

I enter the Void, and I am shocked to see that it is not empty or nothing or void of anything at all. It appears to me as a place full of colors! Imagine emptying endless buckets of paint in countless colors into an atmosphere with no gravity. I pass through the Void in awe of all the countless floating colors.

18

Releasing Grief

It is late 2004, and I just turned forty-six years old.

I have started dating again, and my new girlfriend is active and athletic like me, which makes me happy. I have had a lingering chest cold for the last six weeks. We tried to go for a run on our first date, but I couldn't keep up.

I have a long history of getting colds that would drop down deep into my chest and just stay there for weeks and weeks. This happens maybe three times a year every year for as long as I can remember. My girlfriend suggests I see her nutritionist. I have never seen a nutritionist before. I believe I eat well and take good care of myself, but what could it hurt? So, I agree.

I meet Katherine. She works out of her house. I fully expect her to analyze my diet and give me dietary suggestions. She is working with some sort of machine I have never seen before and touching my fingers. She stays silent, occasionally peering at me over the top of her reading glasses. There is an awkward silence—like one of us wants to say something but neither of us is speaking.

And then she blurts out with confidence, "You have grief trapped in your chest that is related to your mother and early childhood."

Well, this was the last thing I ever would have expected a nutritionist to say, but somehow, deep down, it rings true. I tell Katherine that my mother was in a near-fatal car crash when I was an infant (we lived in Stockton, California, at the time), and while she was in the hospital recovering, I was sent to Seattle to live with various relatives. When my mother and I were finally reunited many months later, my mother swears I didn't even recognize her.

At the same time, I have no actual memory of this. I was only about four months old at the time of the accident and then around one year old when we were reunited. So, while on some deep level this feels true, my mind is insistent that I can't possibly be sad over something I can't even remember!

Katherine simply hands me a homeopathic remedy called "Lung" and asks me to follow the instructions on the bottle for dosage. Then she asks me to let myself cry whenever I feel sad.

The first part, following the instructions for the dosage, is easy. But the second part, letting myself cry, is hard. As a stalwart type, I usually override grief, sadness, or tears anytime I feel them coming on. Anger, I can express. Laughter too. Grief, not much at all. But I do know that I often tear up when watching sappy movies—especially ones with little kids.

As I get ready to leave, I want to know more about Katherine. It turns out she is psychic, although a more proper term today might be "medical intuitive." Her cover is "nutritionist," but in truth, she is so much more. The awkward silence at the beginning of our visit was her silently checking her intuition to see if I would be able to hear what she wanted to tell me. She tells me that some people just won't hear something that sounds a bit weird or "out there," and in those cases, she simply offers nutritional advice.

So I go home and start purposely seeking out sappy movies, and when the tears start to well up in my eyes, I try to open and really let them fly. It takes a long time and lots of practice, but I finally get the hang of it. Something so easy for others is something I really have to work at.

I start to really enjoy it. I cry and I cry. My face gets all red and swollen. *So what?* I cry and I cry. Sometimes there is so much grief, my body releasing tears in gut-wrenching sobs, that it is almost epic. Over maybe the next two years, my nasty chest colds start to disappear, and I would guess that over the last ten years they are now 95 percent gone.

The funny thing now is that I have more body awareness. I still don't cry in public or around others in any natural or easy way. It's hard for me. But I can sense what feels like "hairiness" in my chest that alerts me that there is trapped, unexpressed grief. When I feel this coming on, I seek out another sappy movie and cry away.

I still visit Katherine every now and then. She is a fascinating person with an extraordinary number of abilities and gifts. I wonder just how many others like her are out there.

To all you other "undercover healers" out there, thank you!

19

Weeping Willows

It is the New Year 2005, and I am having a dream . . .

I am fishing on a large flood-swollen steelhead river on a cold and lifeless gray day. There is a stiff south wind blowing, and ragged shards of icy rain are pelting the river valley. I wade in and start fishing by working my way downstream. I have to keep moving to try to stay warm. I see no fish and catch no fish. Filled with a tired, haggard, cold despair, I begin the long, slow trudge back upstream toward my car. But as I come around a long bend in the river, I am shocked to find three brand-new weeping willow trees planted right in the middle of the river! And a short, stout man is leaving the river near the trees, and he looks at me, points to the trees, and says, "These should really improve the fishing!" With a mischievous smile and a twinkle in his eye, the man disappears into the forest.

I am a serious fisherman, and I knew that trees planted in the middle of a river would indeed "improve the fishing." Big fish would take up residence underneath the big trees and find shelter from the river's heavy flow. But this impish, old man had not just planted any trees . . . these were weeping willows. Somehow, I knew that allowing myself to grieve and to feel grief and sadness were important to my inner journey and that it would indeed "really improve the fishing."

I was becoming a sort of mystic fisherman who used dreams and visions to catch things in the unconscious. And I was learning that an honest, free, and open expression of feelings would help my fishing!

20

Spiritual Boot Camp

It is January 2005, and I have signed up for a year-round spiritual study group. I'm back to working with Brugh again. He calls this year-round group "Joy's Jubilation." We all call it "JJ" for short. I am joined with forty others, and we will meet in person four times a year at a place called Rex Ranch near Tucson, Arizona. We will also have weekly and monthly tasks online and a private dream forum.

Being in the throes of the wild and unexpected Kundalini energy, this group helps me feel contained and gives me a sense of community. I'm hoping to be with peers who can sort of hold my hand while I'm going through all of this. I'm super excited to be here and looking forward to going deeper into my journey and to being more serious about understanding what is happening to me. But I'm shocked by the structure Brugh has created for our time together as well as for the year ahead:

4:30 a.m.: Get up
5:00 a.m.: Honor the body (exercise, walk, yoga, dance, etc.)
6:00 a.m.: Meditation
7:00 a.m.: Morning session (meditation and group work)

8:30 a.m.: Breakfast

10:00 a.m.: Second morning session (meditation and group work)

12:30 p.m.: Lunch

2:00 p.m. to 5:00 p.m.: Free time

5:00 p.m.: Meditation and group work

6:30 p.m.: Dinner

8:00 p.m.: Meditation and group work

10:00 p.m.: End of day

I am not used to so much meditation and group work. Nor am I used to getting up at 4:30 a.m. (which is 3:30 a.m. Seattle time for half the year in Arizona). The entire retreat carries a palpable buzz or energy that feels like caffeine in the air. Each night, I go to bed exhausted but cannot sleep a wink. I lie down and just buzz and doze; deep, restful sleep eludes me. *Are we really expected to keep up this same routine when we get home?!*

I have a high-pressure job as CEO of my own company, which is starting to grow and become profitable again after being mired in enormous debt for many years. I am still a single dad with two kids and actively involved in their lives. I have started dating too, and I like being with my new girlfriend. Plus, I like to sleep!

Brugh said we could opt out and get a partial refund if it was all too much. It is. On the last day, I get up in the morning, my mind made up. This is too much for me. I will tell everyone I can't continue.

I arrive at our first morning meditation in a sad state. I really wanted to be a part of this group. But after what felt like four straight nights of no sleep, I've had enough.

During the meditation, I feel depressed. I am pondering this when a woman with jet-black eyes appears and sits right in front of me (this taking place in my mind's eye). She has her hair in a ponytail and a coffee in her hand. It looks like she got up, threw her hair in a ponytail, grabbed some coffee, and rushed over to see me. I silently ask her if she is encouraging me to stay in JJ. She answers yes by showering me with a wave of what feels like "orgasmic honey." This is a very physical sensation of such thick love and pleasurable warmth that I can scarcely believe it.

In that moment, I change my mind. I decide to stay.

I'm so glad I did. I figured out a way to make the schedule work for me. I ended up working with this group for two years, and they were some of the most rewarding, interesting, and intimate years of my life.

21

Marrying Unison

I am having a dream . . .

I am with a woman.
> *She is young and beautiful.*
> *I playfully toss her over my shoulder.*
> *"I know you like me," she says, "but it will be my sister that you will marry, not I."*
> *"But I have not met your sister."*
> *"You will."*
> *"But where, when, how?"*
> *"Be patient. For now, you only need to know her name. Her name is U-N-I-S-O-N."*

Many years after my Kundalini awakening began, an expert on Kundalini told me that the goal of all Kundalini awakenings was "union with the Divine." Maybe that was what this dream was portending.

22

Unity Football

I am having a dream . . .

I am sitting in a large horseshoe-shaped football stadium at night. The place is packed—completely sold out and rocking with energy. My seat is up high, deep in the horseshoe.

It is a neutral field, and the fans here are split evenly—the north side rooting for one team and the south side for the other.

As I gaze upon the nearly 100,000 energized screaming fans, time suddenly stops, and all the fans instantly morph into giant rose quartz crystals. Each and every one of them pink and with a bright light glowing brightly from within.

Such a feeling of UNITY and BEAUTY and BLISSFUL PEACE, and communal UNCONDITIONAL LOVE in that moment.

And then time returns, the place is rocking again, the rose quartz crystals lit from within recede and morph back into fans screaming and cheering for their teams.

Such a gorgeous dream experience of what felt like duality (opposing fans) and unity/nonduality where we really are all One. I loved dreams like this and the sense of immense gratitude I felt in experiencing these different states would carry over into my waking hours for many days afterward.

23

The Love of Mary

I t's a cold and gray Saturday afternoon in February 2005. My new girlfriend, Shonagh, and I have an entire weekend alone. We both have two children from prior marriages, and this is the first time in our short three months of dating that we've had an entire weekend together without our kids.

We have enjoyed our dating time together thus far as sort of fellow voracious spiritual seekers and students—churning through new books and new experiences.

We met a few months earlier at a Thanksgiving party held by mutual friends. I arrived at the party early. She arrived a bit later, and as she walked in the front door and zipped by me, I felt all the hair on my body stand up—she was hot, but this was more than that. There was a palpable electricity between us that felt almost paranormal. We began dating almost immediately after the party.

Now we are in my bedroom at my home. We have a copy of Ram Dass's book *Be Here Now* and are perusing all the various spiritual exercises in the back of the book entitled "Cookbook for a Sacred Life." There are practices for postures, breathing, yoga, meditation, eating, sleeping, dance, renunciation, and many more. I suggest it might be fun to just randomly open the book and whatever page we open to that will be the exercise we try. Shonagh agrees—that would be fun. We will let the universe choose for us!

I close my eyes and randomly select a page and find myself staring at a practice of Sexual Tantra. The exercise seems fairly straightforward—it is an exercise in devotion. We are supposed to make love, but instead of keeping the pleasurable sensations for ourselves, we are supposed to selflessly offer up every kiss and every sensation of pleasure as an act of devotion to a divine being.

Shonagh loves and prays to Mother Mary, and I am still in the middle of a full-on Kundalini awakening and my entire life seems somehow involved with all things Divine Mother/Divine Feminine. So we decide to devote our lovemaking as an offering to the Divine Mother.

We begin.

We make love. I try hard to offer up all the pleasurable sensations I am feeling. It's nice, but if something is supposed to be happening, it isn't. At least not for me. This goes on for about twenty minutes.

Shonagh is physically attractive, and I decide that I don't want to do this selfless devotional stuff anymore. I just want to have good old mortal human sex with my girlfriend. But as I go to say something to her like, "Can we just have regular sex now?" I look up toward the ceiling and there is Mother Mary hovering above us and looking down on us with immense love. I have high cathedral ceilings in my bedroom, and Mary is up near the ceiling.

I am generally not clairvoyant while awake in the middle of the day, but there she is, as clear as day, in our bedroom. It is most definitely not some wispy apparition.

She is in, what I think is called, her light body, and she appears to me as most of the Catholic depictions show her to be—she is about five feet tall and wearing sky blue and white robes with her head covered. Yet she also appears to me as bright light.

Shonagh has her back to Mary, so she can't see her. I want to loudly exclaim, "Mother Mary is in our bedroom!" but before I can say anything, Mary enters my body. The experience is shocking on all levels.

First of all, John, as I knew myself to be, is swept aside and was diminished, like a tiny pea in the throat area. This aspect of John is demanding, "What the fuck is going on?!" and he is terrified.

At the same time, some greater presence is aware that my body is suddenly filled with an ecstatic love, maybe a thousand times greater and more pleasurable than any drug. Orgasms pale in comparison. But this ecstatic love is too much—my body is screaming that it is going to somehow explode, that every circuit is on overload and about to blow.

But Mary had work to do.

Mary completely takes over my body. Every single pore in my body exudes Mary's immense ecstatic love into Shonagh. Mary cradles Shonagh's face and looks at her with immense love, and a veritable torrent of ecstatic love flows from my eyes into hers.

"John" still remains shoved aside—a mere trifling pea in all of this immense and unexpected grace-filled drama. And the greater awareness is full of warning—my body is not constructed to handle all this immense, ecstatic love. Just when I am certain the body will blow up, it ends. Mary disappears. The entire experience lasts maybe ten or fifteen seconds.

Shonagh is in tears. I share what I saw and what I experienced. I share that Mary loves her. I mean *really* loves her.

Shonagh says she felt it and that "no human being has ever looked at me like that."

I feel graced beyond belief. I feel awe having experienced the vibration where divinity resides. I realize with certainty that the vibration I generally live in, and that of most of humanity is in, is so far from the divine vibration of ecstatic love that it's probably a good thing most of us don't touch it or experience it while having our human experiences.

The next day Shonagh awakens in the morning, and her first thought is to "get the fuck away" from me. The entire experience shook and frightened her. We had only been dating for three months.

She shares with me that she is thinking, *Do I really know this guy? Who is this guy really?*

We don't break up, but for the next two weeks, she spends countless hours weeping. At the time this happened, she was doing CrossFit and running and doing triathlons, but for the next two weeks, she could barely walk for more than ten minutes at a time.

A few months later she and her two daughters move in with me and my kids and we end up getting married and blending families. We stay together for the next ten years before going our separate ways. Today, Shonagh is a remarkable spiritual teacher who very much embodies the Divine Mother in all her work.

24

Wake Up!

I am having a short dream . . .

I see two nature spirits—they look like tiny green human dragonflies. They are each holding a pair of cymbals. They slam them together in unison and yell at me, "WAKE UP!"

What if the process I am in now—a person who identifies as a man and who is primarily oriented toward a masculine way of being in the world—is now in a process of finding and discovering, perhaps even rediscovering, his feminine nature? And what if a part of that feminine awakening is rediscovering a deeper connection to nature, to nature spirits, to Mother Nature, and indeed to the body itself?

25

Thai Connection

It is a warm summer evening in 2005. Last night, I took my kids and some of their friends out to a Thai restaurant nearby that we all like. There is a particular Thai waitress who works there that I am somehow connected to. She is beautiful.

I am discovering that heart-centered meditation often allows and encourages strangers and others to open up to me in random places. On one occasion, this waitress felt compelled to share with me through tears that she had to leave her six-year-old boy back in Thailand. She carries a sadness in her eyes that I am powerfully attracted to.

Last night was no different. She spent an inordinate amount of time at our table. I could feel the energy dancing between us. She would stand or kneel close to me, and I could feel immense love flowing between us. I could have just closed my eyes and basked in it.

A few weeks later, I am back at the Thai restaurant with my kids and stepchildren, my wife, and my in-laws. There are eight of us seated at a large table. The beautiful Thai waitress comes to our table and begins to take our drink orders. She moves to stand directly behind me.

Suddenly, I feel a large three-foot-wide tunnel of energy that barrels up into my body and then out the back of my heart chakra directly into our Thai waitress! She just stands there while it flows upward through my body and then into hers. Time seems to stand still. I am bearing the intense energy. This Thai waitress is normally *very* talkative, but this time she is silent for a good ten seconds. Then it is over. Conversations return, and everything is normal again.

This is becoming a semi-regular thing—whatever all this Kundalini energy is doing to me, it also occasionally spills out and into others in a very unpredictable fashion. I never know when or where or with whom this will happen. And I never know what to do or say afterward. I feel somehow that I (and others) am being healed and graced by the energy, but in truth, I don't really know what it is or what it is actually doing.

26

Angel Circle

For the last month or so, a little voice has been saying to me, "Go hold space in one of Jennifer's Angel Circles." Jennifer does weekly Angel Circles where she teaches others to work with their guides and angels.

I contacted Jennifer a few days ago and asked if I could practice holding space in one of her circles. I wasn't exactly sure what it meant to "hold space," but I was pretty sure that was what I saw a man named Paul do in our circles with Brugh. He seemed to just sit there intensely focused on sort of holding the group together with an invisible, energetic net. In any case, it felt like a selfless thing to try.

Jennifer is so fun to be with—totally in touch with her magical child and she "sees" fairies, angels, guides, and all sorts of stuff around people. She said, "Sure!" and asked me to come Thursday. So I did.

I get there a few minutes early and sit in the car, heart-centering. She is holding this Angel Circle lunch in the back of a bookstore, and I feel anxious and awkward going in. I find her and the group and take a chair in the circle. I am the only man in a group of eight women.

Jennifer has us all introduce ourselves and state why we are here. When she gets to me, I simply say, "I want to practice holding space in a group, and Jennifer offered to let me try here today."

The circle begins and I try to hold space. To me this feels like a deeply feminine place—a state of unconditional love. But it also feels impersonal. It's a sort of warm, embracing, compassionate safety net. That's the best way I can describe it.

Just a few minutes into it, Jennifer stops and says she can see a pink band of light exiting my heart and running through everyone in the room. While I am happy something is actually happening, I am also miffed, as I wanted to try to blend in and not be the center of attention.

I last only about five minutes before the endless chatter of my mind kicks in:

This is stupid.
What a waste of time.
I wonder what Jennifer's shadow is.
That redhead is a bully.
Tell her all YOUR stories, John.

It goes on and on and on.

I fight with the voices. I start trying to force the feeling of holding space. The voices continue:

You suck at holding space.
You should be participating too.

At the same time, I acknowledge the work Paul does in holding space for Brugh's groups:

He does this for how many hours, how many days, how many groups?
Damn, this is hard work!

An elderly woman next to me begins talking about her difficult medical history. She is having a really hard time in her life now. I settle down a bit. I let my inner voices chatter away and try to do the best I can.

I just sit here for about an hour feeling pretty open, letting something move through me and letting the voices chatter away. Weirdly, I definitely feel something moving between me and the elderly woman, and it helps me keep focus.

Basically, I just sit there and sort of surround everyone and absorb everything.

Our time is nearly up now, and Jennifer leads us through a guided meditation to close. I fall into it very deeply. She then asks us all to return from our meditation, and I come back very slowly, almost grudgingly.

Jennifer then asks me how my meditation was. I tell her I fell in very deep. She then asks if I have seen the movie *Spider-Man*. I say, "Yes. It's one of my favorites."

Jennifer then says that when she first opened her eyes (while mine were still closed), she saw four "light workers" standing behind me. Their light was pouring into me and through me, and from my heart center, an infinite number of "webs" connected everyone in the group, and these webs extended all the way up to the heavens. She said a disproportionate number of the webs were flowing to the woman next to me with whom I had felt a connection.

Wow!

At this point, all the women in the group start thanking me. They say the healing energy in the room is so thick you could cut it with a knife, that it feels wonderful. Many said they could feel it flowing through me.

Wow again.

I give Jennifer a hug, thank everyone, and leave, feeling both elated and a bit embarrassed.

I recall meeting a man once, and I watched him work with a vexing problem a woman had. I was stunned at how little he did. He said very little and always gave her the power.

I later asked him what he did for a living. He said he was a shaman. I asked him what he did as a shaman, and he said, "I mostly hold space."

Huh?

At the time I didn't get it at all. But now I see just how much is going on when one opens, stays present for others, lets the divine flow through, and just sort of gets out of the way.

27

Fairy Heaven

As the Kundalini energy seemed to take over my body, I learned that the body often goes through a great many unexpected and unpredictable physiological changes and adjustments. This can manifest itself as all sorts of weird symptoms.

At one point I came down with miserable body aches and a fever. It might have been just a normal cold or flu, but it felt different. The fever had a sort of delirium aspect to it, and, in the afternoon, I took a nap and had the following dream:

> *A strange sort of Yoda-like creature with a short, stout body and a head like a deer says to me, "Breathe pranically." Somehow, in the dream, I know how to do this, and start breathing pranically. Then the creature says, "Open your mouth wide." I do this, and he sticks his entire head way down my throat and has a look all around inside me. Then he pulls his head out and says to me, "WONDERFUL! All your channels are open!*

I'm so sorry it took me so long to get here, but things aren't so organized in fairy heaven."

The next day all the strange symptoms start to fade.

28

Modern-Day Superhero

I am having a dream . . .

I see a good guy—Superhero Turtle, like a Teenage Mutant Ninja Turtle—sitting with other people near the front of a moving train.

At the back of the train, the door flies open and Bad Guy— who looks a fusion of Yosemite Sam and the Tasmanian Devil— is yelling and making a ruckus. He wants a confrontation with Superhero Turtle.

Superhero Turtle sees Bad Guy, but instead of confronting him, he walks downstairs into a basement where he meets Wise Turtle sitting cross-legged on the floor. Superhero Turtle sits cross-legged across from Wise Turtle.

They sit quietly as if meditating.

Superhero Turtle coughs. Something is coming.

And then Superhero Turtle vomits all over the floor.

Wise Turtle begins to eat the vomit and says, "Mmmmm, it's quite good actually."

As I see it, this dream shows the friction between what appear to be opposites. Superhero Turtle only identifies with the good and can't possibly see that he contains the forces of the bad guy too. But our superhero maturely chooses not do battle with Bad Guy. He knows that this potential confrontation on the train is also taking place within him.

So, he goes deep. He goes down and finds a wise guide. Our superhero can't contain both these forces, so he vomits up his shadow—the bad guy.

But Wise Turtle is larger and has more access to a wider range of forces and perhaps isn't so identified with just one identity—neither the good guy nor the bad guy.

Superhero Turtle can't contain or integrate his shadow. But he found a wise elder who could. And that wise elder resides within him.

29

I'm Sorry, I Love You,
Please Come Home

It is the summer of 2005, and I'm with my new wife, Shonagh, on a tour of sacred spiritual sites in England. The first night we spend at the Hilton in London, and on the second day, we meet all the people we will be touring with. There are about twenty-five of us from all over the world. I love them all. All but our tour leader. Ugh.

"Gale" is a big woman—maybe six feet tall with a large head and big, broad shoulders. She is mouthy, blustery, and incredibly self-centered. She's like a passionate Italian on steroids but with none of the fun or joy. Not at all what I had expected from a tour group leader of sacred spiritual sites. She seems like she hates men and makes it clear that she hates George Bush and that he is one of "them" (controlling, global-elite patriarchal men), and she has no problem cussing up a storm.

I can't stand her—which is bad because Gale is also very intuitive, empathic, and clairvoyant, so I'm sure she just *knows* how much I can't stand her, and I feel like I can't hide it. I avert my eyes every time she looks at me.

I go to bed that night determined not to let her ruin my trip. I am suffering from jet lag, and England is experiencing a once-every-hundred-years kind of heat wave (it has been one hundred degrees daily for almost an entire week), and the hotel we are in tonight has no air-conditioning. It's not like I am getting any sleep.

I had heard of a Hawaiian healing process called *Ho'oponopono*, and while I wasn't even sure I understood it properly, I decide to give it a shot. I try to imagine our tour leader as a part of me—like a long-lost soul part—and that I was going to invite this part of me to return home. I was about to invite the part of me that is mouthy, blustery, self-centered, and loves a good conspiracy theory back "home."

I'd been working on integration and pulling back projections, and I'd seen amazing things happen doing this kind of work. Following what I learned from that and from my limited understanding of *Ho'oponopono*, I create my own little ritual.

In the sweltering darkness, I place my hands on my heart center and invite in the experience of unconditional love. I imagine a loving space, and then I bring up the image of our tour leader, Gale. With as much sincerity as I can muster, I say to her, "I'm sorry. I love you. Please come Home." Over and over, I look at her in my mind's eye and repeat, "I'm sorry. I love you. Please come Home." I do this for maybe a full hour. Finally, I drift off to sleep.

The next morning, I see Gale. Everything has changed. I genuinely like her. And she genuinely likes me. We joke and laugh. We hug and throw our arms around each other like longtime pals. The sudden transformation is striking. We go to dinner that night, and she cusses out George Bush, and it doesn't bother me because now I like her and think she is funny. She pulls me aside and says to me candidly that all the men who have come on her tours in the past have always been gay and/or conspiracy theorists. I am neither, and she tells me that this is new for her.

Maybe because of my little ritual at night I begin to really appreciate her and feel compassion around her. I hear her tell her own life story—especially about her relationship with her father—and the horrid words he said to her when she was about thirteen years old. I feel compassion for her and wonder if maybe something about her childhood experience with her father has caused her to hate men. I wonder if all her mouthy bluster is just fear and insecurity.

Gale takes us all to a crop circle and asks us to meditate in the circle. The women all sit down and begin to meditate. I can't seem to sit still so I spend maybe a half hour walking in circles around all the women, and instead of meditating, I quietly hum and chant. Afterward, Gale practically runs up to me and thanks me for helping her and all the women feel safe so that they could go deep in their meditation. I honestly didn't know I was doing this, but maybe, somehow, in connecting with Gale deeply in my little ritual, we had found a deeper connection, and I was actually helping her now.

On our last day, Gale takes us all on a private sunrise tour of Stonehenge. It occurs to me that what she is doing must be hard and that it takes courage to take a bunch of unknown people from all over the world to tour sacred sites and handle all sorts of crazy logistics, and that they may or may not have any wondrous spiritual experiences. So, I walk up to her and whisper in her ear, "Thank you for organizing this tour. It must have taken a lot of courage."

Her eyes tear up and she whispers back, "Thank you for saying this. You have no idea how much it means to me."

I went from absolutely hating Gale to accepting her. Appreciating her. Feeling compassion for her. Even wanting to help and assist her.

I did have some amazing spiritual experiences on this trip, but this one might have been my favorite and the most enduring and practical. I learned so much! I surrendered my judgment and sincerely tried to hold Gale—as me—in love. And, in the process, our relationship changed. She did not change. Not one bit. She was still mouthy, blustery, and self-centered. She still hated George Bush and loved her conspiracies. But *I* changed. And because of that, our relationship changed. And in doing so I was freed. And weirdly, so was she. I felt lighter and freer and sort of giddy.

On the last night, as I lay there in the dark thinking about the sudden and wondrous transformation in our relationship, it reminded me of Jesus who, in Matthew 22 said, "Thou shalt love thy neighbor *as thyself.*"

30

Celtic Priest

I am in Glastonbury, England, in 2005. I am part of a tour group, and we have split up. We have the afternoon all to ourselves, so I go to the ruins of Glastonbury Abbey with beautiful park-like grounds. I am still jet-lagged, so I find a large shady tree and lie down to take a nap.

When I wake up, I realize I only have about thirty minutes before I must meet up with my tour group again. I decide to walk the ruins of the church, although there isn't much left here—just some ragged remains of old crumbling walls. I start at the lower end of the church, and with my hands on my heart center, I walk slowly and reverentially toward the altar.

About halfway to the altar, in my mind's eye, I transform into a priest leading some sort of ritual procession, and I hear a voice say, "Slow down." For about five seconds, I *am* a priest! This sort of unusual experience almost never happens to me when I am awake. I note that I am dressed in what looks like a long, dingy white robe.

Afterward, I gather with my group, feeling really shaken but in a good way.

The next day we are in Glastonbury again, and I am in one of the tourist shops, and I see a large dingy white robe for sale along with other clothing. It is the *same* robe I saw in my vision! A handwritten note on the robe says, "Druid Ceremonial Robe." Then, I walk across the street to a bookstore and find a book on Druids and see illustrations of Druids wearing the same type of white robes. These dingy white robes represent the water element. And the Druids were the Celtic priests! Because Glastonbury Abbey was the remains of a Christian church, I assumed that when I saw myself as a priest, I was a Christian priest from days gone by. But I forgot that the Christians had plopped their church right on top of the Druid site.

Prior to this, I had no belief one way or another about past lives, but now I was more open to the idea that maybe we have lived many lives and perhaps we can remember them.

As if to affirm this, our group had private time early the next morning at sunrise in Stonehenge. We park and walk through a tunnel under the highway that leads from the parking lot to Stonehenge on the other side. And as soon as my eyes set sight on Stonehenge, projectile tears shoot from my eyes. Yet my mind could not grasp any of it. Some part of me is having a spectacular reunion, bubbling and flowing over with memories and strange feelings, while another part of me is completely clueless!

I remember communing with nature, earth, the stones, and the cosmos many eons ago, but the memory is very faint.

31

Emptiness and Bliss

My tour group in England is about to spend the day hiking up to the Tor. The Tor is a hill with sacred ruins at the top in a part of England that used to be known as Avalon. Our day is to be split up into four parts:

1. We go to the Thorn Bush and empty ourselves completely.
2. Then we walk reverentially to the top of the Tor.
3. At the top of the Tor, we open ourselves to the heavens and ask to receive Divine Light.
4. Then we hike down into the woods and ground the Divine Light we received at the Tor into two ancient trees—Gog and Magog.

We begin at the Thorn Bush, which looks just like it sounds. A boring sort of scrubby, thorny bush or small tree. We are instructed to empty ourselves—whatever that looked like or felt like—so that we will be receptive to Divine Light at the top of the Tor.

I close my eyes and sort of grasp the thin thorny branches and small trunk and proceed to try to empty myself. It takes a few seconds because I cannot get over that this Thorn Bush looks like every other thorny, scrubby bush I can see. I can't see anything at all that is special or spiritually significant about *this* particular bush.

But then the strangest thing happens. As I begin emptying (I really have no idea what this means or how to do it—it just sort of happens), I begin to feel simultaneously backfilled by great bliss. The more I empty, the more blissful I feel. In maybe just one minute, I am overwhelmed with bliss!

We hike up to the Tor. Nothing happens. At least not to me.

I open to receive Divine Light. As far as I could tell, nothing happened.

We hike down to Gog and Magog. Nothing happens (although the trees were really cool).

What I learn about myself that day with the "boring" Thorn Bush is that maybe peace and bliss are ever present. That maybe I don't need to go find it, seek it, achieve it, or grasp for it. I just need to let go and surrender and empty myself of the almost ever-present stress, worry, anxiety, fears, negativity, and control.

All those stories about people who go out into the world seeking "gold" only to later discover that the gold was closer to home than anyone knew and that maybe the gold was inside themselves all along make sense to me now.

32

Outed

When my tour group in England arrives at a new crop circle, all the women spread out and sit cross-legged to meditate in a large circle on what looks like a bed of hay. As the only man in our tour group, I am alone. I look around but feel a bit exposed and anxious over the idea of sitting in the middle of some farmer's field. I had been planning to meditate and hoped to connect with the aliens who supposedly created this circle, but I give up on that idea and decide to just walk around the circle and quietly hum to myself.

Afterward, as we leave the circle, a reporter from *The Times* newspaper out of London is standing by our bus ready to interview us. Ordinarily I would have run for the hills—I didn't want people I knew back home to know that I was touring sacred spiritual sites and hanging out in crop circles. I kept this side of myself carefully hidden.

But, heck, I'm way over here in a crop circle in some farmer's field, and no one will read about me in a newspaper from London, so I agree to be interviewed. Kind of like . . . what happens in a farmer's field in a crop circle in England, stays there, right?

"I'm John Latta from Seattle. Yeah, I'm here touring sacred sites like Stonehenge, The Tor, crop circles, etc. I didn't meet any aliens but thought the energy in the circle was quite nice. I truly don't know if man or aliens are making these cool-looking circles. Tourists who come to crop circles are called *Croppies*? OK, then I'm a Croppie!"

And on he goes to interview a gal from our tour group who was from New Zealand and a bunch of others, including Gale, our tour group leader.

Imagine my surprise when I get back to Seattle and a good friend of mine asks me if the John Latta who was in the crop circle that he read about in *The Times* of London was me! And then my brother calls me and asks the same thing!

WTF?! My brother and my friend read the newspapers from London? And they read about tourists in crop circles there?

I sort of stammered and made excuses. I did not want people at home to know about this side of me. Suddenly, I felt naked, vulnerable, and "outed." Ugh.

Generally, I have been a fairly private person. But I find that I have been outed so many times now in so many ways that I have mostly given up trying to hide anything at all about myself. It has been freeing and disconcerting at the same time. But it does seem like we live in an age now where secrets are increasingly hard to keep.

But maybe that is not such a bad thing.

Seems like the truth finds a way out whether we like it or not!

33

Losing My Head

I am having a dream . . .

It is early in the morning. The best time to fish. And I am all alone. I am back on the little dock I learned to fish off of in Los Alamitos Bay in Long Beach, California. But this morning I brought no rod, no reel, and no hook. I am listening closely to the lulling, gentle waves lapping against the side of the dock. I thought I spied a giant orange fish—like the size of a Greyhound bus—swimming below the dock. But there are no giant orange fish in these waters. I lean way out, straining to see down into the water. The gentle waves lull me. Looking. Looking. Looking. For the big orange fish. The waves are so nice and lulling. And then, plop! My head falls into the water. It descends ever so slowly. And out from under the dock, the giant orange fish swims out and inhales my head. It is really quite serene without my head.

All this time I had been overwhelmed with fear, stress, and anxiety. And now I am so filled with peace. So funny. All I had to do was to lose my head.

34

Mayan Priest Giving Light

As part of my year-round spiritual study group curriculum, I am exploring different religious, spiritual traditions, and cultures. Somehow, I come across a website that is all about the Mayan calendar, and the year 2012—still seven years away. I see a photo of the Mayan Ruins at Tulum and feel the hair stand up on my body. *I* don't seem all that interested, but some other part of me and my body were extremely interested!

A while later, I am with a group and participating in one of my first ever shamanic journeys. Here is what happened:

As the drumming commences, I see myself descending a long tunnel. Nothing happens, though there appears to be light ahead. But I choose a side tunnel that suddenly drops straight down. It becomes huge, very wide, and very dark. It is so steep that I am sort of half swimming and half flying.

I become aware that I am in someone's intestines (the bowels of the Earth?). The intestines seem to go on forever. After a very long while, I exit the tunnel at a gray, somber place—like a sodden rain forest and tundra. It is drab and gloomy. I walk around aimlessly wondering why I am here.

Soon I become aware of fifty-foot-tall warriors. They are diffuse, so I can't see them very well. They don't frighten me. I think they are trying to communicate with me, but it's as if we're not on the same wavelength.

On the horizon I spot a bright light. I fly toward it and pop over the distant hillside and voila! Oh my God! I am smack dab in the Mayan Ruins at Tulum. However, the civilization is very much alive here. I alight on top of a tall building where a powerfully built young Mayan greets me. He appears to be preparing me for something. Soon I am surrounded by hundreds of wildly chanting and dancing Mayans.

Then the heavens open up, and pure white light enters through my crown and infuses my whole body. I glow. I am light. With a mighty sweep of my hand, I send light and illumination far across the sea. I watch the light travel out to sea like an immense gust of wind. Then I sweep my hand inland and watch the light race inland toward the hills, illuminating everything in its path.

This was one of what became many visionary experiences I began to have where I was a priest. I saw myself as a Mayan priest, a Druid priest, and even a Catholic priest. I still wasn't onboard yet with past lives as being a real thing, but if past lives were a reality, it was clear I had been a priest many times before.

A priest! How ironic. For my entire adult life, I had been antagonistic toward religions and priests. But maybe I really *had been* a priest in lifetime after lifetime. And maybe, in this lifetime, it was somehow important that I have lots of "real world" types of experiences before stepping back into the more familiar role of the priest.

35

Mary Magdalene Healing

Shonagh asked if I would go with her to a Tom Kenyon work-shop on Sacred Relationship being held in the fall of 2005. I had a meditation CD of Tom's, and I knew he did sound healing work and that he had a nearly four-octave voice; otherwise, I knew nothing about him. But in the interest of my budding marriage, I said yes. I expected five or ten couples sitting in a circle and working on improving their relationships.

But when we got to the workshop, I was stunned to see nearly 500 people in a giant conference room at the DoubleTree Hotel south of Seattle. I was also shocked to see that, while Tom was local (he lived on Orcas Island), most of the attendees were from all over the country and indeed all over the world.

Tom Kenyon? Who was this guy? I didn't know but was about to find out.

For the first day and a half not much happens. It feels like Relationship 101, and I didn't glean anything new. But Tom was a good speaker, funny and grounded. He did do some sound work where he seemed to channel sounds during some meditations, but nothing much seemed to happen. At least not to me.

In the afternoon on the second day, Tom announces that Mary Magdalene is present, and she wants to do some healing work. Tom asks us to close our eyes and says that he is going to do some sound healing (vocal toning) and that if we see anything scary while we have our eyes closed to just "keep on walking."

I close my eyes, and Tom begins his unusual toning. Nothing is happening to me, and I am annoyed because I am sitting under bright lights and am sure that I can't see anything in my mind's eye because the bright lights are penetrating my closed eyelids.

Crap.

Maybe five minutes go by and still nothing is happening; I am mildly annoyed and keep shifting in my seat.

And then . . .

What feels like a round tunnel three feet in diameter seems to open beneath my seat, and what feels like a blast furnace of energy erupts upward into my body with great force from below. My entire body begins quaking, and then I begin to see every single wounding experience in my entire life in perfect chronological order. I see my terror in my first nightmare. I see my anguish when my parents took my baby blanket away from me. I see when my parents made me stay home on Halloween as punishment because I had wet the bed again and the sad, forlorn look on my face as I peered out the window and watched all the other kids out trick or treating. I see myself in a hospital all alone about to undergo major surgery and see a doctor inserting an adult-size catheter into my seven-year-old penis and me screaming in pain . . . on and on it goes. I see dozens of scenes—major and minor "woundings"—each and every one of them a brief three-second movie. At one point about ten minutes into it, my body is shaking and sweating, and the energy stops briefly, and a wordless voice says, *Do you want to continue?*

I say, *Yes. I am tough.* And it all begins again exactly where it left off.

Twenty minutes later, it ends with the final wounding scene —my devastating divorce four years earlier. Through it all, I saw it and "kept on walking."

My body is exhausted, and I am sweating profusely. I am simply stunned at what has taken place. Not only did the intense energy that blew into my body completely exhaust me, but the sort of life review of *all* the various wounding and difficult experiences in my life was incredibly draining.

I feel graced. I am devastated. And I am incredibly tired. I need a shower and a nap.

Later, after the weekend with Tom Kenyon was over, my wife shared with me that a voice had spoken to her on the first day that said, "John is not here for the information. He is here for the healing." How right she was.

But what was actually healed? Why was it necessary for me to review *all* the wounding experiences in my life again? Looking back, I have a sense that I had one last look at them all, a chance to learn and claim the seeds of wisdom from each and every experience, and then to move on. Over time, it is like somehow the memory of all those experiences is dead and gone, having faded into the sunset. Somehow it seems to me that healing is just that—a chance to claim the wisdom from each and every experience and then to get unstuck and move on.

To learn. To grow. To claim the wisdom. To feel the love. To embrace the experience. Then to move on. And then to not look back.

Whatever sort of tentative conclusions I have drawn about this experience with Tom Kenyon and Mary Magdalene, to this day I remain awed and mystified by what we loosely call *healing* . . . how it happens, when it happens, and the various transformations that take place over time afterward. I'm also mystified by why sometimes healing doesn't happen—as if the various "woundings" serve a purpose as well, and until that purpose is fulfilled, no healing is forthcoming.

36

Embracing Death—Part One

This month, November 2005, my year-round spiritual study group is exploring the mystery of death. We were asked to prepare for our death. Put our affairs in order. Make a will if necessary. Make amends to others if necessary. Say what needs to be said to others before we pass on as if we really were leaving.

I am enjoying this immensely. I find it incredibly freeing to embrace death and to unencumber myself. Having had an epic fear of death just a few years earlier, I am loving facing what was once my greatest fear.

We were also asked to read books about death, listen to music CDs on death, and to meditate on death. In short, we were being asked to not run from death but to move toward it and to embrace it.

This morning I am meditating on death. While meditating, a woman's voice speaks to me and says, "Before you know more about death, perhaps you should know about life," and I am presented the following dream:

I meet a woman with deep-blue eyes. They are very loving eyes, though they are like large, unblinking, bottomless blue crystals.

She takes me to a Spanish-style home at the edge of a forest. We go to the second-story exterior entrance set on a spacious round porch, a corner of the building. An old, massive wooden door—like the door to an ancient mansion—opens and beckons me to enter.

White light with a tinge of blue spills out of the open door. I enter, and I am bathed in the light. I am Home. My entire body tingles with peace and bliss.

The light turns to a whitish yellow—like early morning dawn—and I see two men: One is Jesus—naked, standing tall, firm, and resolute. Attached to Jesus from the waist down is what looks like his conjoined twin brother. But his twin looks like Hercules—all brawn, sinew, sweat, and muscle. He, too, is completely naked. The Hercules-like twin is struggling mightily to get away from his conjoined brother, but he and Jesus are connected, and Jesus stands firm.

In an instant, the Hercules twin stops struggling and looks over his shoulder. For the first time, he sees his divinity. Jesus and Hercules stare into each other's eyes and then passionately embrace.

This was my first experience of truly beginning to understand what it means to be both human and divine. It felt as if the dream was showing me that the Hercules twin represented the human body identity and/or ego, but the Hercules twin later realized his divinity, which was represented by the Jesus twin. Perhaps what we call *life* is the union of human/body and the divine. Maybe when the Hercules character was unaware of his divinity, life was a struggle, and he wanted to go his own way. But, in truth, when he recognized his divinity, he realized that he was in service to it and not the other way around. And when he recognized his divinity, his identity changed, and boundless joy resulted.

37

Embracing Death—Part Two

During my exploration of death, I have been having an increasing number of dreams where I am about to die—in most cases, I am falling from the top of a mountain or high cliff, and while falling I say, "Why can't I just die before I die?" and, as if this were a magic incantation, my fall slows considerably and I land on the ground, light as a feather.

I'm curious about this. What might it mean to "die before I die"?

So I go into meditation, and I ask with sincerity, "Please explain the mystery of nonphysical death and resurrection," and I am presented with the following dream:

I am in what looks like a farmer's field. It feels like a cold October night, and the field has already been harvested. There is a large harvest moon looming low on the horizon.

At the edge of the farmer's field, I encounter a skeletal human figure, like a scarecrow. It is a forbidding sight—a partially clothed, decaying human skeleton-scarecrow mounted about ten-feet high. It looms over me, almost daring me to move forward.

But I do move forward fearlessly, and I walk past it to a patch of bright moonlight. I bow before the moon. She comes to me, and we embrace. Then she fuses with me. I turn into a silvery liquid that looks like mercury. I flow like a small river of mercury across the top of the Earth on into the distance.

I come to what feels like the end of the Earth and flow off into the deepest black space drop by drop. "I" disappear into this pure blackness of space. The nothing. Infinite darkness. I sit here for what feels like a very long time.

And then I become what looks like a gigantic golden grid surrounding Earth. Like a spider's web, I am the grid and ever expanding, becoming more intricate and more complex. Such beautiful geometry! Yet this web is formed by what looks like millions of human beings holding each other like an impossibly large group of linked skydivers.

As I feel into being this human grid, I sense that others come to it for solace and support.

What did I learn about nonphysical death and resurrection?

That perhaps the only thing that dies is "me" and that in the death of "me" one is somehow reborn or reconnected into something far larger. Maybe the only real death is "me" into "we." Somehow the path to nonphysical death and resurrection is one of facing, embracing, and going toward one's fears with great faith, trust, and surrender. One then "dies" into something far greater. The "me" is still there, but so is the "we." Maybe this is also the path of transforming from feeling alone and selfish and full of fears into one of selflessness and service that transcends all fear.

38

Let the Salmon Be Your Guide

I stand waist-deep in the river
Heavy under a sullen gray sky
Pockets bulging with the shiny faces
I thought I had to wear
They are no more
I reach for the river
The accumulated rust and crust
Pours from my pockets
The flies to tempt big fish jauntily float downstream
They are no more
I let them go—it's OK
Next come the credit cards
And the driver's license—I'm not sure about these
And then my last nine photos
They are no more
They all swim in a seesaw motion
Riding the current to the bottom
But I can't let them go
Status, permission, memories

They are no more
Desperately, I dive to the bottom
Grasping for cards, photos
That bounce just out of reach through churning rapids
I give up the chase
They are no more
Suddenly, I see the salmon returning home
Males with cruel teeth and ragged scars
Powerfully pulsing upstream
To spawn and die
And be no more
How nice to be a salmon
I swim with them—naked
I sense wisdom, purpose
Mystery is just around the bend
For me, alas, it is no more
A still, gray mist descends upon the forest
I have no house, no car, no family
No clothing, no friends
Where will I go now that
I am no more?
The bewitching hour
The river speaks in her soft loving voice:
"Let the salmon be your guide.
They know the way Home. You are blessed, John.
For you are no more."

I wrote this poem in 2005 trying to capture the immense loneliness and sense of loss and fear I sometimes felt as I was undergoing a completely unpredictable major life transformation—one that didn't seem to have any known specific timeline or goal. For all the grace I was feeling and experiencing, there was also great fear and a sense that who I had known myself to be was slowly disappearing and dying a long, slow death.

39

Accepting Eyes

While on a tour of the Mayan Ruins in the Yucatán in 2006, I met a woman from Ireland named Irene who had the most amazing eyes. They weren't beautiful, luminous, or piercing. Instead, they were just so *accepting*—perhaps even unconditionally loving. It did not matter who she was with. And it didn't matter if she agreed or disagreed with the conversation. Her eyes were *always* accepting.

I have found that my natural way of dealing with other people when I'm feeling defensive or argumentative is to intensely focus my gaze. It feels like my eyes are both throwing out daggers and lifting a protective shield.

So, I try shifting my attack-and-defend eyes to Irene's accepting eyes. I imagine I am looking at other people through her eyes. Almost instantly, I find I am in a state of listening and supporting and being fully present instead of attacking and defending! Simultaneously, I can feel that in making my eyes completely vulnerable, that I am taking my "self" out of the exchange. And, in that state, I feel so amazingly present and undefended!

Trying on a different set of eyes shifts everything!

40

I Don't Have to Do It This Way Anymore

I am in Tulum on the Yucatán Peninsula with my wife and our four kids. It is early in the morning. Dawn. I am having a dream . . .

I knew something important was happening today. I could feel it.

The Mayan priests, thirty of them in all, wake me up at dawn and take me to the edge of the Caribbean Sea. They look resplendent in their beautiful, lush robes made of thousands of peacock feathers.

They ask me to disrobe and enter the sea.

Is this a baptism? Or some ancient Mayan ceremonial rite?

I leave my clothes on the beach and walk out about ten yards from shore. The water is crystal clear and pleasantly warm—and very shallow, so I just sit down.

I wait.

The Mayan priests watch me intently.

A reef shark swims up to me and bites me. Hard! It gloms onto my leg and will not let go.

I let it chew on me a bit. There is blood and pain. But strangely, I am not concerned. In fact, I say to myself, "I don't have to do it this way anymore."

I pull the shark off my leg and give it a nudge. Again, I say, "Yep. I don't have to do it this way anymore."

And then I swiftly and purposefully swim out of the shallows and dive down into the deep blue sea with the Mayan priests all cheering wildly behind me.

This dream stuck with me for years. Time after time. I would look at my life and how I was living it and tell myself, "I don't have to do it this way anymore." Very slowly, over time, I learned to intuitively listen deeply within and respond from there rather than waiting for pain and suffering to move me.

41

Seeing Michael

I am in an advanced energy class with maybe about ten to fifteen other people. I was invited to join this group, but it is clear that they are far more advanced than I am. They are all clairvoyant—they see energy around people and things. I don't see anything. I want to, but nothing is happening.

We are doing an exercise, and I finally just give up on seeing energy around others. I close my eyes and relax. Suddenly, even though my eyes are closed, I see the person next to me (a young, cool software developer with a braided beard who works at Microsoft) and am stunned at what I see.

He is seated on a chair, and it looks like a sword of white light is protruding downward from his butt and attached to it are eight other "swords" of white light aiming outward and downward in what looks like a gorgeous chandelier made of light. The entire form is moving; it goes down, then up, then back down again, hesitating, twitching, then up and back down again. It never stays still. It is indescribably beautiful.

I open my eyes, and I am *so excited* to share what I saw! I actually saw something! I tell the group what I saw.

Without missing a beat and speaking with all the enthusiasm of someone who is maybe commenting on the weather, the teacher says, "Oh yeah—that's Michael. He has a terrible time staying in his body."

As I am driving home, I note the upwelling of joy I feel. I got to see Michael beyond his outer human form at a depth I'd never seen in anyone else before. It felt as if I'd seen the divinity in another for the first time ever. I am filled with immense gratitude.

42

High and Low

It is 2006, and I am having a dream . . .

I am bouncing up and down—from the Colorado River in the depths of the Grand Canyon up to the top of the Canyon where a 500-foot-tall White Buddha is perched. I look the White Buddha in the eyes briefly and then fall all the way down to the bottom of the canyon, and then repeat up and down. I fall to river and then bounce up and look into the eyes of the Buddha. Over and over. Up and down, and up and down.

In so many ways, this is what the mystic path feels like to me. I bounce high and stare into the eyes of eternal wisdom, only to fall back to Earth again as a regular Joe. I live as a regular Joe for a while and then soon I bounce up and stare again into the eyes of great wisdom, compelled later to try and live the wisdom. It's enthralling and sometimes exhausting.

43

A Living Oracle

Over the last six months in late 2006 and early 2007, four different people have told me, "You should get a reading from Bella Karish." I've never had a "reading" of any kind before, and I don't know anything about it. Nor have I heard of Bella.

But they all implored me, "She is a living oracle. You better go fast—she is ninety-six years old!"

I take it as a sign and look up Bella. She is in Southern California near the Burbank airport. I regularly fly to Southern California on business, so I schedule a session with her, and three weeks later fly into Burbank.

I enter a dark, old building, and an older man guides me into a back room.

I meet Bella. She looks sweet and elderly and has a sort of joyful, teary-eyed effervescence about her. As I touch her hands, I note how pudgy and pillowy soft they are. I sit across from this sweet elderly woman, and she launches into her reading with a deep, loud, and confident Russian accent that assaults me:

"You are a monk and reverend from the past. You have come to help and heal. Now, you are going to start a healing center, and

113

you are going to make people very happy. You are going to sell your business. You are not a businessman anymore. You have touch for health—when you touch people, they feel better. You are here to raise people up so they can be better, better, best!"

She goes on and on. I'm happy with what she is saying about me. It's nice. But I've never had a reading before, never seriously considered past lives, and wasn't sure I was ready to give up my business yet. I didn't know what to make of all this.

Then she turns up the volume. This sweet ninety-six-year-old Russian woman is now practically yelling at me. "YOU ARE NOT BELIEVING THIS! BUT IT'S TRUE!"

She could see the deer-in-the-headlights look in my eyes. She then launches into my "Three Selves." Bella explains that everyone has a male and female aspect, a high-self aspect, and a cosmic-self aspect that she calls the Three Selves.

My male aspect is Lester: Lester is a leader. Grounded. Practical.

My female aspect is Grace: Grace is a bestower of grace.

My high-self aspect is Alexander: Alexander is a "helper and defender of men."

My cosmic-self aspect is Melchizedek: Melchizedek is a "metaphysical priest forever."

She talks about various colors, crystals, and stones that would be beneficial to me. She talks to me about various family members and my ex-wife and my children. But over and over she keeps coming back to my selling my business, moving, and starting a healing center, that I am a monk and reverend from the past who has come to Earth to help and heal others.

When it is over, I leave and call my wife from my cell phone and tell her a bit about the reading. I'm both excited and overwhelmed.

When I get home, I mention again that Bella thought we would move and start a healing center. We had just done some minor remodeling on our home, the house was paid off in full, and I had no intention of moving. None.

But my wife says, "I would love to have a big organic garden."

The house we live in now is too shady to have a garden. Still, I won't budge. We are not moving. My daughter, Kelsey, is fifteen years old now and is listening to our conversation. She goes online to look at homes for sale in our neighborhood.

"Hey, Dad, come look at this home for sale."

"No. We are not moving. Hey . . . I know that place. It's gorgeous. It has a pond in the backyard and is only a few minutes away from here. Let's go look at it. But we are *not* going to buy it—we can't afford it, and we are *not* moving."

We all bundle up in the car and go to look at the home for sale. It's on five acres and has a nice sunny exposure. Perfect for a big organic garden. Dead center in the middle of the backyard is a pond—maybe a half-acre in size that has fish in it and is deep enough to swim in. There is a large island in the pond with two tall cedar trees on it. There is a bridge to the island. It is May, and the entire place is blooming with flowers, green grass, and lush, healthy trees. It looks like a magical nature sanctuary even though we are mere minutes from town and the freeway.

Twelve years earlier, my children and I were living in a tiny rambler on Education Hill in Redmond, and I had gone out for a bike ride and saw this very same place for sale. I remembered thinking it was the most beautiful property I had ever seen in our general Redmond, Washington, area. And here I am marveling again at the beauty.

The pond. Oh, the pond. I *love* water and the prospect of having a big pond with rainbow trout in it and that I could fish in and swim in is compelling.

Still . . . I had been through a brutal recession and divorce in 2001 and found myself mired so deep in debt then I never thought I would get out again.

Beauty or not, I still will not even consider moving. Debt is the enemy.

The next morning, I get up early to meditate and have the following vision:

I see myself meditating on the island in the pond at the house we looked at yesterday. As I sit there, a giant teardrop made of light about three feet across falls from the heavens and enters the crown of my head, flows through my body, and enters the ground beneath me.

I go to tell my wife this has happened, but before I can speak, she says, "You know that house we looked at yesterday? I had a dream where a goddess was in a boat in the pond there and it was all misty—it looked like the mists of Avalon—and she was waving to me and beckoning me to come with her."

I tell her about my own vision, but I'm still not ready to budge. They look like signs, but I'm still fearful of debt.

But the dreams and visions continue. The next day in my meditation, I see what looks like a Mayan pyramid on the property. I also see what looks like a French gardener and his small garden shed, and he tells me he is the caretaker of the property.

I start to soften. The home has been on the market for six months and has already come down in price. Maybe the owner would consider coming down further in price.

The realtor takes us back to look at the house again. I leave everyone in the backyard to walk in the front yard, and I see what looks like a small rodent scurrying ahead in the grass. I think it might be a small rat. But it suddenly freezes and allows me to walk right up to it. It's not a rat. It's a small wild baby rabbit. It lets me gently stroke the top of his head between his ears. I've seen thousands of wild rabbits, but none of them have ever just let me walk up to it and pet it.

I go back to tell everyone that a baby rabbit let me pet it, but the realtor calls me over and says to me that there is something magical about this place. She points out that her Cavalier King Charles spaniel is playing with a swallow. The swallow is swooping back and forth over the realtor's dog, and the dog and bird are having a fun time. This goes on and on. I've never seen a swallow play with a dog before! Nor has a wild rabbit ever allowed me to pet it before.

I soften some more. I contact the owner, make an offer, he comes way down in price, and we buy the place and move in. I'm back with a mortgage again and a large one this time. Ugh.

But I also felt a lot like Kevin Costner's character in *Field of Dreams*. I'd had signs, visions, and dreams that seemed to be saying, "Buy it and they will come." It was a leap of faith, and I took it.

Twelve years later, in 2019, I met another Russian woman named Eugenia Oganova, who did readings and was unusually gifted. She explained to me that there is a grid made of light that surrounds Earth and that this grid is helping Earth and humanity ascend to a new higher dimension. She said many beings are involved in constructing it. She said the grid touches down on Earth in many places, and wherever it touches down, there is a greater sense of harmony. And one of the places it touches down is the island in my pond right here in Redmond!

I have had visions of this grid, and I knew that I and this property were somehow connected. Others (besides me and Eugenia) are also aware of this grid touching down here too. For example, a teacher of Peruvian Shamanism visited here once who was gifted with a sort of "knowingness" (he was not visual), and he walked right out onto the island in the pond and declared, "There is a portal here." He stood about three feet away from where I had that first vision of the giant teardrop of light entering me from above in my meditation.

In addition, I'd had dreams that a giant "aquifer" made of light was under the property here. The pond was fed by a deep underground spring, and I wondered if the light grid that touched down in the pond sort of fed light to the spring as well. In my mind's eye, it looked like a giant earthworm made of light. I had seen that, from this deep underground pool of light, various vertical columns of light seemed to connect the pool of light with the heavens and that these columns of light were in the middle of our family room!

My wife and I did create a sort of healing center and have had thousands of people come here for all manner of events, gatherings, circles, teachings, and healings over the years.

Grid of light or not, there have definitely been times my life did *not* feel harmonious, but swimming in the pond—a pond that is weedy and sometimes has leeches in it—is always remarkably restorative to me. The island itself is like a portal of peace. If it didn't rain so darn much here, I would be in the pond or on the island every single day!

I love to travel and love the sense of newness and discovery that taking a new road or new trail stirs in me. But I love home too, and this home, this slice of land, and this pond—even after fourteen years—still feel like a sanctuary to me.

44

Going Home

I've been having a lot of dreams with the same theme. In these dreams, I am usually in a vacation type of spot—on a beach swimming or snorkeling or maybe even at a ski area. In all the dreams, it feels like I'm having a ton of fun. But, in every dream, a woman comes up to me and taps me on the shoulder and says, "John. It's time to go Home."

I always stammer and cry out, "No! I don't want to go Home!"

Over and over it's the same. "John. It's time to go Home."

"No! I don't want to go Home!"

After what felt like dozens of these dreams, I have a final culminating dream . . .

I am in a big, busy city. It is almost time for me to go home. For the first time, I give in and decide that I will go home now. I take my box out from the building I was staying in onto the street. The box is long and rectangular—perhaps twelve-feet long and two-feet by one-foot wide.

As I'm standing there with my box on the busy street, I look at my watch. It's 2:30 p.m. Though it is not quite time for me to go Home yet, I decide to leave early and beat the traffic. So, I grab my box and prepare to leave, and "poof," the city and the building I was staying in are gone.

I am way out in the country, and all I see before me are three paths—a left, a right, and a middle path. All paths appear to go off into meadows and gentle hills. I see lots and lots of people on the left path—it's almost like a freeway—and the right path is mysterious, shrouded in dark smoke and clouds, and hard to discern. There are people here too but not nearly as many as the left-hand path. The middle path is completely empty—there are no people on it, and it disappears far off in the distance.

I choose the middle path. I grab my box and head down the middle path with no idea whatsoever where I am or where the middle path is leading me. Just me and my box going Home.

And just like that, all the dreams of being sad, angry, and resistant because it is time to go Home come to an end.

I am going Home now. I accept this. And my path the rest of the way, perhaps for the rest of my life, is the middle path. It's lonely. There's no one else on this path. But, somehow, I still manage to pop over and occasionally hang out with others on the left-hand path and on the right-hand path. Both.

But what exactly is this dream implying? Is it yet another message about staying centered in oneself? About avoiding extremes? About not getting caught up in left or right, good or bad, right or wrong, and dark or light anymore?

I did not know it at the time, but a long period of what felt like loneliness, emptiness, dispassion, and an ever-shrinking bucket list lay just around the corner.

45

Healed in an Instant

I t is the last Saturday in August 2007.

Shonagh and I plan to get up early on Sunday, drive all the way to Winthrop (a four-hour drive), and go for a long hike. The kids all start back to school the following week so this will be the end of summer vacation and our last chance to get out and hike before the craziness of school, homework, and after-school sports and activities sink in.

But during the day, I hurt my knee while working in the yard. It swells up a bit and is really sore. I don't usually get knee injuries so I try to walk it off and stretch it, ice it, and rest it, thinking it will be no big deal, but nothing helps. It is so sore that I don't think I will be able to drive four hours, hike all day, and then drive four hours back. I am truly bummed because we had not been hiking all summer, and this would be our last chance.

I go to bed hoping that some rest is all I need and that it will be fine in the morning.

But when I wake up at 5:00 a.m., my knee is just as sore as the day before with some extra stiffness thrown in. I try to walk and loosen it up, but nothing works. I have a knee injury, and the last chance to hike of the year will have to be canceled.

I am sitting on a kitchen chair in full on dejection. I needed this trip, this road trip, this hike before the crush of back to school. Road trips and hikes in the mountains feed me.

While sitting dejectedly on my chair alone in the early morning light, something strange happens. It feels like a big bucket of etheric water above me is poured on my head, penetrates my body from head to toe, and somehow my knee injury is flushed out. It happens in like two seconds, and I know my knee is all better.

I stand up and test it. It doesn't hurt at all. I can scarcely believe it. I test it by walking, stretching, and even jogging a bit, and it is fine.

I grab my wife (who was still sleeping and who maybe wasn't as enthused as I was about a four-hour drive, a six-hour hike, and then a four-hour drive back all in one day), and in thirty minutes we are on the road!

All day long, I keep testing my knee, and it's totally fine. We have a great drive and a great hike in warm weather on the sunny, dry side of the Cascades.

How to account for a knee injury that gets flushed out with a sort of "etheric water" and is healed almost instantaneously? Why do things like this that border on the miraculous sometimes happen, and other times they don't? When things like this happen and other "miraculous" healings occur, I get excited and am sure I see all the solutions to our nation's healthcare problems. But then the next time my knee hurts, it seems it must heal the old-fashioned way. Why?

Who or what is behind healing—if it happens, how it happens, and when it happens?

46

Dream Books

I t is 2008, and I am having a dream . . .

I am staring at the cover of a book entitled Unmistakable Life. *It looks like a large hardcover book. It has a dark-violet cover, and the title is in ancient gold script lettering. It feels like a book full of deep wisdom and revelations, and I am very drawn to it.*

I go to Amazon to order the book, but it's not listed. I search elsewhere on the internet but can't find a book by this title. This is the first time a book has appeared to me in a dream that has not yet been written. I think, *Maybe someday I will write it.*

The title is alluring and mysterious. If the title is *Unmistakable Life,* then somehow it implies that life itself can be mistaken. What does this mean? What is an "unmistakable" life?

One day I sit down determined to channel the book. And all I can get to, is that an unmistakable life is a life of "the union of the liver and the lived."

So, who or what is the *liver* and who or what is the *lived*? Might it be life lived in union with God instead of feeling separate in the ego? Or maybe a union of me with life?

I don't know, but the book still haunts and guides me and pushes me in the best possible way.

Another dream . . .

I am staring at the cover of a book entitled Surrender to Freedom. *The cover is of a sunset on a partly cloudy day late in the afternoon. The sun is low on the horizon and is illuminating the underbelly of the clouds in a spectacular sunset. The title is set at the bottom of the page in black letters. Again, the book is alluring.*

Again, I wake up and go to Amazon and look for it. Nothing. I search the internet. Still nothing. Again, I am haunted by the title and the cover photo. Again, I wonder, *Am I destined to write this book?*

And what of surrender as a path to freedom? What does that mean?

Over the years there were more "dream books" that appeared to me that had not yet been written:

- *Avatar: A Beginning*
- *2020–2060: Beyond Oz*
- *The REAL Descent*
- *The True*

Are these books I am destined to write? Or were they some sort of downloaded information? I don't know yet. But the titles of the books are compelling, and they all exert a great magnetism on me.

47

Meeting Pleiadians

My wife, Shonagh, has been mowing through books about alien cultures such as the Sirians and the Anunnaki. The books are all channeled material from the Sirians about changes taking place on Earth and their recommendations for how to live through the changes. She wants me to read the books.

I look at one, and it sounds like a dumb conspiracy-theory book. It is full of information about how we are controlled by the Anunnaki—an ancient reptilian race full of cold, power-driven masculine forces. It has lots of recommendations—get rid of your TV, your microwave, and stop going to McDonald's, etc. I don't like this book at all, and it causes friction between my wife and me. I defend my TV, my microwave, and my cheap lower-vibration food.

Then she begins reading a whole bunch of books full of channeled material from the Pleiadians—an ancient alien culture of light workers helping bring about the changes taking place on Earth. I am just not into any of these channeled alien books.

About this same time, I become enamored with a book called *The Reconnection* by Dr. Eric Pearl. Dr. Pearl was a chiropractor who, after many years of practice, suddenly and inexplicably began channeling healing energy through his hands. The healings were extraordinary—there were amazing physical healings, but his patients would often begin channeling voices and strange energetics.

I love the way he writes. He is flamboyant, spontaneous, and irreverent. Not the usual spiritual-healer type of writer! I look him up and am happy to discover that has an upcoming workshop in Seattle. While I am not sure I am called to be a hands-on healer, I like him. So, I want to go. Plus, there have been many times where spontaneous healings and energy passed through me—often very dramatically—through my hands. If nothing else, I know that Dr. Pearl is living his life in a very present and spontaneous way that I know is important for me to open to. I also just want to meet the guy because he seems so darn funny!

That night, I pick up Eric Pearl's book again and randomly open it. Shonagh is devouring another Pleiadian book. The chapter I randomly turn to in the book is about Eric searching for answers. He was consulting all sorts of folks. What is this new healing gift he has now? A psychic woman in Beverly Hills was walking him through a sort of journey where he was ultimately to ask his question. To make a long story short—the answer he got was that he had three strands of DNA. Eric was not satisfied with that answer. He is a doctor and firmly stated that all doctors know there are only *two* strands of DNA. The psychic woman told a different story—originally, we humans had twelve DNA strands and apparently the bad aliens found a way to disconnect ten of our twelve strands. Those with three strands have come back to this planet to share light and information. And those with three strands are *Pleiadians*!

Mind you, Shonagh is sitting next to me devouring her Pleiadian book, which I wanted nothing to do with. Up until a week ago, I had never even heard of Pleiadians. And now this new author who I love is being told that he is a Pleiadian!

I can't begin to tell you how many times now that I found myself pushing against something (in this case aliens here on Earth) only to be immersed in it.

So, we go to Dr. Pearl's workshop, and there are a lot of people here—maybe a hundred or so. I'm still a bit weirded out, but I try to learn his new energy-healing technique.

While there, I feel a strange attraction to a woman who is there. Nearly everyone there is with a friend, partner, or spouse. She is alone. I can't get over the attraction I feel to her. During a break, I even mention it to Shonagh and point her out in the crowd.

A few minutes later, I am chatting with some other folks, and the mystery woman walks right up and introduces herself to me. It turns out she is highly intuitive and knew I was talking about her behind her back.

I stammer back and forth in awkward conversation. I ask her what she does for a living. She calmly says she used to be a pharmacist but now she does "Pleiadian light work"!

This Pleiadian phase hangs around in my life for a while. I have no idea if Pleiadians are real but do sometimes have experiences in bed where I feel paralyzed and what feels like dozens of ET-like long, slender fingers are being gently pressed into my body. This happens a fair number of times, but while I am open to whatever is happening and trust it, I also want to *see* whoever or whatever these beings are!

One night, I lay there in the dark and mutter, "Why can't I *see* Pleiadians?"

And instantly a group of voices says back to me, "We're right here, John."

I have been having so many odd experiences for the last few years that I was learning to just roll with them all. But this was hair-raising—even for me. Mind you, I am not asleep, not dreaming, and the voices sound like they are all in bed with me. But I see nothing.

I never got to meet Pleiadians (at least visually) and can't say specifically what they did to me. My encounters with them faded, but I do still have a fondness for that cluster of stars in the sky called *Pleiades*.

48

Dropping in on Nostradamus

Shonagh is now reading a book about Nostradamus, the famous French seer and physicist who lived in the 1500s and recorded all sorts of prophecies. I fall asleep next to her and quickly slip into a dream . . .

It is night. I see a man with a heavy beard in what looks like an old wooden cabin. Somehow, I know this is Nostradamus. It is nighttime, and there appears to be some light coming from a fire in a fireplace.

Nostradamus sits in a wooden chair. On his lap is the upper torso and head of a human body that is facing him. This head and torso somehow appear to be alive, and Nostradamus is silently communicating with it.

I look up, the ceiling opens, and an immense energy is pouring down from the heavens into the crown of Nostradamus's head—as if the entire night sky is being funneled into him. I see eyes in it and know that the energy has consciousness.

I wake up a few minutes later and tell Shonagh I have just met Nostradamus. I describe his cabin and his appearance, and she tells me it was him. She shows me an illustration of him that matches the man I met in my dream.

I am intrigued by prophets, seers, and prophecies. Somehow, I think the dream was trying to show me how Nostradamus was able to see the future. While I have had a small number of prophetic dreams myself, I never do figure out from the dream how Nostradamus received the information.

49

I Want to Walk in God's Shoes

I am in Egypt in 2008 with Shonagh and a group of about thirty people led by Tom Kenyon. We are all touring various sacred sites. Tom is a world-renowned sound healer, and I'd had a profound experience in his presence back in 2005. I'd never been to Egypt before, and Tom was guiding us to sacred sites here.

Tom booked us private time in the in the King's Chamber in the center of the Great Pyramid at Giza. We form a line, and we each get two minutes to lie down alone in the King's crypt. Tom explains that we can ask for anything we want and that the King's crypt can grant wishes like a high-speed time machine.

There is a sort of hazy, altered vibe here. I feel like this is an amazing opportunity, but when I get my turn, I have no idea what I am going to ask for. I climb in and lie there and eventually say, "I want to walk in God's shoes."

We leave the pyramid, and when I am standing outside, I close my eyes and, in my mind's eye, see what looks like an endless string of upright dominoes stretched across the entire Sahara Desert. The domino closest to me falls over, and an entire chain reaction takes place.

I'm a bit fearful about what I asked for. It appears I have set something big into action.

50

Selfless Service

My dreams are about to take me into a Jesus phase. It begins with this dream:

I am looking into a pregnant woman's womb as if via ultrasound. I see an infant—it looks like it is maybe eight months old. The infant looks me in the eye and then points a tiny finger up to the sky and says to me, "I and the Father are One."

I was tremendously excited by this dream and knew it was some sort of Bible quote. (I looked it up; it is John 10:30.) It seemed to imply a coming Oneness, and this excited me. A few months later, I have another dream:

I am outdoors in a very dark place late at night. I observe dark and violent soldiers riding out on horseback to crush something. Further ahead, I see two men standing on either side of Jesus. Jesus is nearly a full-grown man but scaled down a bit so that he looks to be only about four-feet tall. He is dressed in white and has a very bright shimmering aura around him of radiant white light. Jesus wants to go out and do good works in the world, but the two men take him into a hidden closet to hide him from the approaching soldiers.

About a month later, I am in Egypt, and I have this dream:

I see Jesus, now a full-grown man, in bed awaiting a goddess. I see a life-size statue of a large buxom goddess. It suddenly comes to life and joins Jesus in bed in a royal union.

A few days later while in Abydos in Egypt, I dream:

I see Jesus Christ crucified on the cross. I am crucified on the cross with Jesus as well. The center of the cross is directly over my heart center.

Upon my return home from Egypt, I have another dream with Jesus in it:

I am with Jesus Christ and his disciples at the Last Supper. I get up to leave and walk around the front of the table, and as I do, Jesus says to me, "John, you are wearing the wrong shoes." I look down but wake up before I see what "wrong shoes" I am wearing.

This was my final Jesus dream:

I am told that I am in Jesus Junior High School now, and I am learning a wide variety of subjects. And I am told that Jesus Junior High School can be very difficult on relationships.

I was tremendously excited about these dreams but didn't really know what to do with them. They seemed to portend something. It was a few years after my year-round study group with Dr. William Brugh Joy, but I was still in touch with him. I asked him about the dreams. He said that the dream where Jesus and I were both crucified on the cross was a symbol of selfless service.

It had always frustrated me that Brugh could see things I could not. Having a sharp, logical, and argumentative mind, I would argue with him constantly in our group, and he would say things like, "Perhaps you have not yet heard the sound of one hand clapping. It's OK. You have time." On one occasion, he said, "John, I would not be so patient with you if I didn't think your destiny was selfless service." *What?* I didn't know if that was a backhanded compliment or what, but it did shut me up.

Selfless service. Sounds good. But do I truly know what it means? Or what it portends?

No. I don't.

Like most folks, I tend to see service as charity, helping the poor or the elderly or the infirm. I think of saints like Mother Teresa. And I think of "selfless" service as existing only to serve others with not a care in the world what might be in it for me.

But I think there might be many ways to be of service that are somehow "selfless."

What does it mean to serve? Who or what is being served?

And what does it truly mean to have no "self"?

It is a mystery that I am still uncovering.

51

Cosmos Man

I n the summer of 2008, I begin experimenting some more with shamanic journeying. I buy a book by Michael Harner called *The Way of the Shaman* and a couple of his CDs with shamanic drumming music. Today I am going on a journey to meet my destiny. The music begins, and in my mind's eye, I ask to see my destiny and picture myself entering deep into the Earth via the pond in my backyard. This is what I experience:

> *I see myself as a fly-fisherman walking downstream alongside the Madison River in Montana just outside the west entrance to Yellowstone National Park. With the river on my left and following a trail next to it, up ahead, I see a simple arch/portal covered with plants and vines. I walk through this arch/portal and am greeted by happy green nature spirits that look like tiny human dragonflies.*
>
> > *Suddenly, I realize I have transformed. I am an old sage, walking very slowly, and it seems as if all of nature is there to greet me and love me. It feels like I am beaming out immense love to all of nature and all of nature is sending that love*

back to me. I have a smile on my face that I can't suppress. I am wearing a cape that trails far behind me. The cape is not made of cloth but of energy, and it contains the entire cosmos. Planets, sun, moon, comets, stars, dark and light, plants, rocks, animals, fire, water, past, present, future, etc.—it's all there. I walk slowly in a state of immense joy—both loved and in love, and I am surrounded by vast love.

As I turn back toward the portal/arch, a nature spirit takes a single strand of gold thread and begins to wind it around and around me. Soon I am in a giant white cocoon, glowing brightly from within.

If this experience of being the wise, old sage in a state of immense love is to be my destiny, I cannot be happier. But, at the time this journey to see my destiny took place, I did indeed have the feeling that I had entered a cocoon. As elated as I had been to see my destiny, I'd forgotten that the cocoon's purpose was to give a caterpillar the opportunity to go through its long phase of dissolution and transformation before emerging as a butterfly.

An exceptionally long phase of what felt like limbo, purgatory, endless waiting, and feeling stuck had begun.

52

Who Am I?

A book I ordered from Amazon arrived and, with it, was a second smaller book, *Who Am I?* by Sri Ramana Maharshi, which I did not order.

Who Am I? proposes a system of self-inquiry where one asks ceaselessly, "Who am I?" and as thoughts arise, one asks, "To whom do they arise?" The goal is to realize the Self—that only awareness remains, and that the nature of this awareness is existence-consciousness-bliss. Through this self-inquiry, one can realize oneself as this awareness.

It sounded easy, so the next morning I resolved to meditate, and as thoughts would arise, I promised myself I would keep asking, "To whom do these thoughts arise?" So, I sat down and closed my eyes and very shortly I had a vision:

> *I see myself standing on the edge of the Earth at dawn—a simple human silhouette backlit by the rising sun. And then a great wind blows, and I see myself start to dissolve—as if I am made of grains of sand—and little by little, I disappear until I am gone. But I realize another part of me is still here watching*

the "me" that blew away and disappeared. In that moment of seeing that I am the one seeing, I feel great bliss.

The next day I resolve to sit and practice self-inquiry again in meditation, and again, I have a vision:

I see myself standing on a city sidewalk. I reach for my wallet, pull it out of my back pocket, and open it. Out of my wallet, a geyser of colorful flower petals erupts, and I am quickly buried in a ten-foot-high pile of beautiful flower petals of all shapes and colors. Then a mighty wind blows, and both me and all the flower petals disappear. Again, I am aware that although I and the flowers have all disappeared, there is still the "me" that is watching and aware of this, and again I feel peace and bliss.

On the third morning the same thing happens—I sit and close my eyes and again have a vision:

I see myself as a monk in a red robe. And then it is as if I melt and disappear, leaving only the robe behind in a lump on the ground. Again, I notice that even though "I" disappeared, there was still the "me" simply watching all of this unfold.

I never really did get around to much self-inquiry, but somehow, in my own way, I got what the book was trying to impart. Some part of "me" is always aware, awake, and watching.

I sometimes beat myself up for reading too many books, but experiences like this one have taught me that many books carry a story, a teaching, a vibration, and a power that never ceases to amaze me.

When the student is ready, the teacher appears—sometimes in the form of a small book that was never even ordered!

53

St. Francis Comes Home

Shonagh invited me to go with her to visit a couple who have a farm up on the North Fork of the Stillaguamish River, east of Arlington. It is a warm and sunny summer day in 2008, and the plan is to pick raspberries and have a picnic lunch.

I meet Jim and his wife, Sherry. They seem like a sweet young couple, and they take my wife and me on a tour of their farm and the old cabin they live in.

Jim then takes me for a walk around the entire twenty-five-acre farm. As we walk and talk, I become aware that Jim has a profound connection to nature. The land is still mostly undeveloped, and he shows me the woods, a small pond and creek, and tells me about all the wildlife that lives there.

Jim is a big, burly guy with biceps the size of tree trunks who works in construction when he is not working on his farm and re-modeling their cabin. His skin is deeply tanned and leathery.

But, as we walk and talk, he just comes alive talking about the land and the animals. There are hundreds of birds here (he puts out something like 1,000 pounds of wild bird seed a month), and he seems to know them all. He tells me that he talks to them and that they talk to him.

Then he takes me over to the cabin that they are remodeling and shows me where he had started to do some work on the foundation and that a mother rabbit spoke to him and asked him to stop. Jim poked around and discovered that she had a nest of baby bunnies under the cabin.

On and on Jim goes sharing his communication with and love for animals, birds, and all of nature. He thanks me for listening to him as he says, "I can't share this stuff with my construction buddies."

As we continue to walk and talk, I am amazed—Jim feels like some sort of reincarnation of St. Francis of Assisi in the body of a big, burly construction guy!

Over lunch, I suddenly become very sleepy. This sudden wave of sleepiness has become sort of a regular thing with me. I seem to be more "open" than usual, and this new openness requires a lot of naps.

So we leave after lunch, and I am so sleepy that I can barely drive home. Even though it is midafternoon on a warm summer day, I climb in bed and crash.

Almost instantly, I fall asleep, and I am in a dream . . .

A stern, solemn old man who looks like a priest is facing me. He is holding what looks like a pushpin full of a purple liquid. The old man then forcefully plunges the pushpin full of purple liquid into my heart and, at the same time, looks me right in the eyes and loudly exclaims, "ST. FRANCIS OF ASSISI!"

I wake up. I am no longer sleepy.

Not long after the dream, I bought a statue of St. Francis, and it sits now at the base of an old cedar tree in my backyard. When I am quiet and still, I can feel the spirit of St. Francis and his innocent, open love for all of nature.

54

The Bardo

I am having a vision while meditating . . .

A powerful masculine voice announces, "The Bardo." I am in deep, black space and see nothing but black. Then faint wisps of gray smoke appear out of the blackness. Then I see what looks like a rectangular metallic structure/sculpture with a pyramid in the middle of the infinite blackness crowned by the sun. Flanking both sides of the pyramid are beautiful wave-like swirls.

I explored the Bardo a bit online and found it to be a description of the death process and a sort of intermediate state between death and rebirth. In some ways, it is experienced like being in limbo. Maybe this is another way of describing the experience of being in a cocoon.

My hope is that I will be blessed with the opportunity to experience this transformation from life to death and rebirth consciously while still alive. The structure born out of the void seemed to speak of full ascension—the pyramid crowned by the sun.

55

God Sound

I am lying in bed at night having a vision . . .

I hear a sound that sounds like "God"—an indescribable sound that seems to encompass "All." And then I see a dark planet in deepest dark space zapped with light and watch as thousands of tendrils of light race around and encompass the planet, illuminating the entire surface.

I wake up with my heart pounding in awe of what feels like the immensity of God. Who or what is zapping celestial bodies with light, light that seems to be alive and have a conscious intent? And why do I find the vision of tendrils of light racing around and encompassing a dark planet way out in space so enthralling and enlivening?

56

What is Light?

I'm having an online discussion with a funny, whip-smart, Jungian-trained psychologist. He is telling me that when someone experiences great trauma through things like illness, divorce, the death of a close family member or spouse, violence, etc., it is called a "Descent Mystery." That, on occasion, one sort of descends into a valley of darkness and a journey into hell and suffering.

But immediately after the discussion, I feel compelled to meditate, and it is as if someone or something wants me to know that what my Jungian-trained friend described is not a descent at all.

I see light from above me descend deeply into my body, and then suddenly, I am staring at a book entitled The REAL Descent. *The book has a peachy-pink color, and the title is in red script lettering across the bottom of the book cover. It seems to be telling me that the real descent is when light from above descends deeply into the body—all the way down to the root chakra.*

What is light?

On another occasion, I am enamored with a few books by Adi Da Samraj, who claims to be the "Avataric Incarnation of Conscious Light." And then I meet him in meditation . . .

Adi Da appears with his hair pulled back in a high ponytail, making him look something like a Samurai warrior. He throws something at me that looks like snowflakes or grains of sand made of white light, and when they enter my body, they make me feel tingly all over.

Is the light from above that descends into the body somehow different from the light Adi Da threw at me?

What is light?

I am meditating . . .

I see the top of my head crack open. I feel like a tiny pea looking up from the bottom of a giant crevasse in my open skull. As I look up, I see light—conscious, alive, silky smooth waves of dust-like particles like a serpent from above moving slowly down into my head. The light slowly and seductively "paints" all the dark spaces in my head. I feel a subtle bliss.

What is light?

I am meditating . . .

I see a woman standing next to me, and she enthusiastically says to me, "Oh, this is going to be GREAT!" Then a giant ball of white light from above me crashes down deep into my body. As if my body were a multistory house, I see that the light has settled in a small room made of light within a much larger sort of underground basement living room.

I go into the small room of light, but a voice says to me, "It's premature," and I back out.

What is light?
While lying in bed one evening, I have a vision . . .

I see "Source"—a pale-blue and white twisted mass—like a giant ball of yarn that is made of pulsing light out in the deepest black space. A strand of the twisted blue-white light shoots out of the Source like a web from Spider-Man and plows into my heart with such ecstasy that it is horrifically painful.

I erupt from my sleep like I have been electrocuted. The pain quickly passes, but fear lingers on.
What is light?
I am dreaming . . .

I see myself walking alongside the ocean. Lightning shoots out of the ocean and plows into the palms of my hands.

What is light?

57

Curbside Temple

It is 2009, and my friend Samantha invites me to Southern California to see Ganesan, the grandnephew of the great Indian saint, Ramana Maharshi. Ganesan is giving a series of talks in people's homes in the Santa Barbara area about growing up with Ramana.

I met Samantha in Brugh Joy's dream forum about six years ago and learned that she is unusually gifted at dream work. I felt it was a gift of grace when she worked with one of my dreams. I've never met her in person, and I have a fondness for Ramana Maharshi, so this is a special invitation.

I fly down from Seattle and stay in a small motel. That evening, I meet Samantha for dinner. She is that rare person with whom I can share my entire expansive mind without her getting triggered or pushing back or politely (or impolitely) changing the subject. We talk for hours and hours. We talk about our lives and all the spiritual mysteries of the cosmos, all the while with our butts on the sidewalk and our feet in Ojai's village streets.

I have learned so much in the last half dozen years and have had so many spiritual experiences, but I still have so many questions. It is so nice just sitting with Samantha, our feet in the street, talking about anything and everything. My journey has often been lonely as I have almost no one I can talk to about my spiritual experiences and insights. It feels really nice opening up.

We have some things in common and a few mutual friends, and we have built up a lot of trust by working on each other's dreams, so it is easy to be with her. Like me, she went through a sudden and shocking spiritual transformation around age forty. Prior to her transformation, she was financially successful, liked what she did for a living, and felt satisfied living a "shallow life." Me too. I don't mean shallow as in materialistic. I simply wanted to get rich so I could retire young and go fishing when the fishing was good and go skiing when the skiing was good. Neither of us expected to go through a complete metamorphosis in our desires and values.

It is night now, and Samantha and I are walking the streets. She asks me to come with her, as she pulls out some keys. She unlocks a door and takes me into a building that looks closed for the night. It is a firm she works at by day, but no one is here now. She turns on the lights and locks the door behind us. She is intent on doing something without asking me about it first. I'm curious and apprehensive.

Samantha plays music on her iPod. "Yes. The Talking Heads are good," she quietly says to herself and plugs in her earbuds. She begins to dance around me with what looks like an invisible needle and thread in her hand. She is like a dancing seamstress and seems to be stitching up tears in some invisible clothing around my body.

"I'm stitching up some holes in your auric field," she calmly says and happily continues to dance and stitch away at my invisible clothing about two or three feet beyond my body.

I didn't know that Samantha can see energy. She is a clairvoyant energy healer!

My wise and intelligent energy-healing seamstress continues to dance around me and stitch me up for the next five minutes or so and then looks me over and decides we are done.

Well, this is weird! But it is cool.

147

Later that night, I go to bed sure that I will have some wild dreams, but nothing happens. I get up and go out to breakfast and then suddenly get very sleepy and head back to my room and crash on the bed.

And then the dream comes . . .

A bunch of Jamaican housecleaners come in and clean out my entire house. Afterward, it is squeaky clean, yet everything is gone. No furniture. Nothing.

I wake up and feel vital, alive, and refreshed.

For the next few days, we gather with others in various homes in Santa Barbara, and we meet and meditate and hang out with and listen to Ganesan. I meet dozens of new and interesting folks. Then I thank Samantha and fly back to Seattle.

For a person who was so determined to live a shallow life, I've always been amazed at Samantha's wisdom and depth. She wrote this short piece on love years ago, and every time I read it my heart melts. Here it is:

Love

When you are able to come to the place where the only thing you wish for and long for, for another person (as the other and for the face of yourself as that other), is the very best loving thing of all possibility for them, knowing you can never know what that very best, loving thing might be—and yet *that* would be your heart-held prayer and gift to them. And then, in turning that inward to ask this for yourself as well: that whatever the very best, loving thing of all possibility, knowing that it is beyond capacity to really know what that might be or look like. Asking that you be able to ask and receive that which is the very best for your soul and surrendering to the wisdom of life to give the offering. Both to another and to yourself. It is to dream the very best for a particular soul, in reverence and humbleness, not knowing what that could possibly be. If you can come to this place, then the "peace beyond all understanding" can be embraced and deeply felt.

Samantha, I will always be grateful that you took the time to invite my loneliness and whirling mind into your warm and accepting curbside temple there in the streets of Ojai. I have no idea what it could possibly be, but I deeply wish the very best for your soul.

58

What Is My Mission?

I am having a dream that is explaining my new "mission"...

I see a tetherball game going on with two competitors both hitting the ball back and forth. I am confused by my role here. Am I one of the players? But then I see my face fused on the tetherball pole as the two people are pounding the ball back and forth.

It was many years later that I caught what this dream was trying to impart to me. That being centered and grounded and holding a sort of "pole" for others to dance around and compete around was a form of service. Some call it "staying Home" or "staying in your vertical tube," and some say it is being "centered" and connected both above and below.

I'm still learning to stay Home, stay centered, and stay connected above and below and still learning that maybe *this* is selfless service.

59

New Discoveries at a Tom Kenyon Workshop

I am on Orcas Island in 2009 with Tom Kenyon and about seventy-five others in a workshop that Tom calls "The White Pearl." I had toured sacred spiritual sites in Egypt with Tom the year before and looked forward to hanging out with him again.

The workshop opens with Tom asking us to release all our anger, grief, fear, inner demons, shit, inner critic, negativity, etc. He says there are beings present with us who will eat the bad stuff we spew out and that to these beings, the spewed out bad energy is like cookies—the beings here love to eat it! He wants us to wail and move and yell and cry and open our mouths wide and let it ALL out.

We begin. Everyone opens their mouths, and there is heavy exhaling and wailing and moaning throughout the room.

At once, some aspect of me shoots straight up out of the room. My butt is still on my chair, but my head is now out in space just beyond the edge of Earth's blue atmospheric band, and somehow, I am sucking all the "bad" energy being expelled into the room by everyone into my body and then blowing it all out of my mouth way out in space. I have turned into a giant metaphysical vacuum cleaner! This goes on for about twenty minutes. I feel a great sense of peace and release afterward.

I can't explain this, and once again, I see how some other part of me simply takes charge on occasion. It's always so unexpected, which I love and feel apprehensive about at the same time.

Now we are near the end of the workshop. Tom asks us to do an awareness exercise. He asks us to still ourselves and see if we can sense the brain sending the message to the lungs to breathe. Then to see if we can notice that *before* the brain commands the lungs to breathe, to see if we can be aware of where the brain gets the command to tell the lungs to breathe. Something happens *before* the brain does its work. The brain gets its command from somewhere. Can we find it? Can we be aware of it?

I sit very still. And I notice it! It's very subtle and swift, but I can feel a signal from my root chakra move swiftly up my spine to the brain, and then the brain commands the lungs to breathe.

I raise my hand. Tom calls on me.

"Does it come from the root chakra?" I ask.

"Yes," says Tom. "Good awareness!"

Oh, yay! I was definitely feeling like the A student in the workshop and pretty darn proud of this new subtle awareness. I continue to be drawn to increasingly subtle things, and I am always amazed at what I'd been missing.

60

Patience and Presence

I t is 2009, and my beautiful daughter, Kelsey, is now seventeen. She has started drinking. A lot. And doing drugs. Lots of drugs. My wife, Shonagh, is angry. I am in denial.

My daughter was such a good, mature, and wise kid. This was the girl all the other moms trusted to be a good role model around their daughters: "Oh, if Kelsey is going to soccer camp, then I'll let my daughter go too." Kelsey was the one who stood up to bullies in school. She got great grades and was diligent in school. She was a wise, old soul in a cute, little girl's body.

So, I'm sure it's just a teenage thing. After all, I started drinking, smoking weed, and partying around that same age too, but it was never a problem.

We find alcohol in her bedroom. I still don't think she has a problem. She gets arrested for being "drunk and disorderly," and I have to go get her out of police custody. I still think to myself, *It's just a teenager thing.*

Then she gets a DUI, and I have to go get her out of police custody again.

She has stopped going to school. I take away her money, her cell phone, and the car keys. Nothing changes. Her friends go from fellow diligent students and athletes to alcoholics and stoners in black hoodies.

Shonagh is not happy about how my daughter is behaving. Her daughters (my stepdaughters) are young (ages eight and eleven), and she fiercely wants to protect them.

The big 2008 recession has bludgeoned my business, and money is desperately tight for us. My company product line has been dropped in thousands of stores nationwide. I am caught up in fear and desperation about our finances. Our big, beautiful dream home on five acres with a pond, which we bought two years earlier, is now underwater by $700,000.

My wife's car breaks down, and we have to share one car—not an easy thing to do with a family of six and no public transportation nearby.

My wife and I explore bankruptcy. She is really angry. I have this sick feeling that if my company goes out of business and we go bankrupt that I will be taking down my business partner, my wife, my stepdaughters, and my own two children.

My daughter's behavior gets worse. Some nights she doesn't come home. I can't sleep. On the nights she does come home, I sneak down to her bedroom to see if she is in bed and I put my face next to hers to make sure she is still breathing.

At one point, my fear and desperation grow so much that I do something I've never done before. I kneel next to my bed and tell God that I am doing the best I can at work and with my daughter and my wife and my stepdaughters but that all the anxiety is killing me. So I just "surrendered." It really was something like, "Jesus, please take the wheel." I surrendered. Fully. Completely. Sincerely.

And then this incredible warm wave of peace came over me like no peace I have ever felt. It was immense peace in a warm blanket.

I crawled into bed and actually slept that night.

My daughter enters a mandated treatment and counselling program. The counselors hint to her mother (my ex-wife) and me that

Kelsey's drug and alcohol problems are BAD and not just a little teenage experimentation and partying. I am still in denial.

Then my daughter runs off, and I don't see her for days. My ex-wife and I try to find her and eventually do. She is living in a sort of party house. The young men there look like they are in their twenties, and they all have excessive black eye makeup smeared all over their faces. They are all scary-looking dudes, and my daughter looks like she is one of them.

We pull her out of the house, and she is like a wild animal, practically hissing and spitting at us.

My ex-wife and I hatch a plan together with our daughter's counselors. We will have her "kidnapped" in the middle of the night and taken to a dual diagnosis lockdown facility and treatment center in Oregon (a three-hour drive away). I am desperately opposed to this. But the others convince me.

We must do this quickly, before she turns eighteen. They won't be able to legally hold her if she is eighteen.

A week later, at about 4:00 a.m., my daughter is kidnapped in the house by a big, burly man and big, burly woman. She puts up no fight, and she is taken to Oregon.

It's a dual diagnosis facility where everyone—alcoholics, drug addicts, and violent kids struggling with things like bipolar disorder, suicide attempts, cutting, and so on—are placed together in one facility. And experts are trained to diagnose what is wrong with all the kids. I quickly discern that if Kelsey had any innocence left at all, being in this facility with her fellow in-patients will be the end of it. I am desperately sad.

My ex-wife and I have to travel to Oregon and back (it's about a seven-hour round trip) every Saturday for six weeks to visit her and for us, as her parents, to get counseling.

Kelsey is defiant. The counselors there assure us that every kid who comes there is initially defiant, but after a week or two they usually settle down and become more compliant.

Kelsey does not. She stays defiant for the entire forty days. There are no apologies. No forgiveness. No healing. No hint that anything at all will change.

We pick her up on the last day, and it is a long three-plus-hour drive home. Our daughter remains defiant about planning any actual changes in her life when she gets home. Then she starts to tell stories about some of the other patients there. Things like how some kids would torture animals because it was the only thing that gave them a sense of power and feeling like they had control of their lives. Again, I feel for certain that Kelsey is no longer innocent about the darker aspects of life, and I feel crushed.

Insurance had covered Kelsey's treatment, and it did nothing. What would I do now? I felt like I was out of options and a dark hopelessness crept over me.

I had heard about a woman named Carolyn Conger, who, as I heard the story, became a parent to her niece at age fourteen and that her niece was hell on wheels—out of control with drugs and alcohol and hanging out with the wrong crowd. But that Carolyn had the gift of seeing how patterns play out over time, and she knew with certainty that the way her niece was behaving and the crowd she was hanging out with were going to be important for her later as her life unfolded. And that Carolyn knew her niece would ultimately be OK. I'd read also about Carolyn in Michael Crichton's book *Travels*. She had a PhD in clinical psychology and was a gifted clairvoyant. (I would later learn that Carolyn was good friends with Michael Crichton and that she was Michael's daughter's Godmother.)

In desperation, I look her up, contact her, and make an appointment.

When we meet, I share that I'd heard the story about her niece and wanted to know if it was true. She says it is and tells me her "wild" niece is now a professor of Creative Writing at UCLA—and Carolyn assures me she feels immense gratitude for that time with her niece.

I ask if she can look into my daughter's future and explain what is going on.

156

Carolyn pauses, closes her eyes for about ten seconds or so, and then says, "Oh, John, your daughter is BEAUTIFUL! She will be fine. Just be patient. In fact, both of your kids will take longer to "cook" than most kids."

I have no idea whatsoever if Carolyn or anyone else can actually know the future, so I remain skeptical, yet hopeful.

For the first few weeks after Kelsey returns home, she remains defiant, and there is no obvious change. But slowly, Kelsey begins to take charge of her own recovery.

She attends court-mandated outpatient classes. She begins to attend AA meetings. She moves out of my house into a dreary, dirty, and messy-looking condo and gets a job at the Hilton Garden Hotel. She drives a beater car.

I try to just be *with* her. To just *be*. We have lunch together most days. Her car barely runs, she has to get up at about 4:00 a.m. most days and drive about thirty minutes to work and is usually off around noon. She seems sad and resigned and yet quietly stoic. I want so badly to try to rescue her and have her be my wise little girl again—the one who was a diligent student, a great athlete, and loved to dance and sing—but my intuition is telling me to just be there and not *do* anything. Let her take charge of her own life.

Patience is not my strongest quality. Nor is patiently watching my daughter struggle and suffer.

She attends AA meeting in Bellevue almost daily. She begins to lead meetings and invites me to a few. I'm sad that all of this is happening but proud of her for leading meetings with dozens of people, most of whom are twice her age or much older. She is diligent about her recovery and continues to go to her outpatient meetings as well.

We talk about her going back to school—she still has not graduated from high school. We see an ad for Maharishi University of Management (MUM), which says, "The school where students meditate." Kelsey is intrigued. The students eat organic vegetarian food and meditate twice a day. It is consciousness-based education. They teach on a block model, where subjects are studied one at a time intensely for shorter periods rather than multiple classes/subjects at the same time spread over a quarter or semester. The school president is Dr. John Hagelin, a brilliant Harvard-trained physicist who I'd heard of. I look it up. It is a "real school" and is accredited.

We go to visit, and Kelsey likes it. I read up on it some more, and a website says it is one of the schools where your kid is *least* likely to get drunk or stoned. With Kelsey still in recovery, this gives me peace.

We hear a rumor that the school won't allow kids with tattoos to attend, and this pisses Kelsey off (her entire left arm is a tattoo "sleeve"), but the school assures us that tattoos are allowed so Kelsey calms down. But before she can go to MUM, she first needs to finish high school. She signs up for a full load of summer school classes, finishes them all, does great, and then begins attending MUM.

Her first year there is hard. It's a small school with only around 1,000 students. The student body is represented by eighty-five different nations. The kids there are generally older than Kelsey, and most are from different countries. Kelsey learns TM® (Transcendental Meditation®) and meditates twice a day in a big golden dome with hundreds of others. It is a shocking change from her life at home.

Kelsey is a certified CrossFit trainer and supports herself by taking a part-time job as a trainer in town at Boom CrossFit.

She calls me about three times a week in tears. It's normal for kids who are new to meditation to have to do a lot of "processing," but Kelsey is also processing an entirely new life and new lifestyle while in recovery while meeting a whole bunch of new friends and attending a school that does things really differently. Plus, the school is in the tiny town of Fairfield, Iowa, surrounded on all sides by miles and miles of corn. It's a completely different environment on all levels for her.

In my twenties and thirties, I managed hundreds of employees as a store manager in multiple stores for a large regional grocery chain, and employees with addiction problems were fairly common. I knew from experience that even if an employee was motivated to quit and be sober, lasting recovery often meant they would need to undergo a drastic change in lifestyle. Among other things, this usually meant new friends, new hobbies, new interests, and sometimes even a new home. The transition time between the old you and the new you—the old way of being and the new way—was often fraught with fear and loneliness, and it could be incredibly fragile. The powerful pull back to the old, familiar lifestyle was often insurmountable. Some employees who became clean and sober were now sad and lonely. In some ways, giving up drugs and alcohol seemed to be the easy part; the hard part was building an entirely new life from scratch.

But Kelsey settles in by the second year and over a six-year period earns two degrees—an undergrad in Health and Human Physiology and a master's degree in Ayurveda and Integrative Medicine.

I was proud of her for staying clean and sober, but I was also unusually proud of her for being brave enough to leave AA. She called me up once when I was on a business trip in Arizona to say that she didn't want to say anymore, "I'm Kelsey, and I'm an alcoholic" because she felt it was perpetuating an identity that was no longer true. She sounded solid. I felt good about her decision. She left AA and never looked back.

When she was at the dual diagnosis facility, her official diagnosis was "stubborn." There was no grand medical and/or psychological disorder. She was just stubborn. Kelsey wanted to do things her way! She always has and still does.

As the years went by, she kept telling me that she never felt wounded or traumatized in any way. She just liked doing drugs and drinking because she felt more like "herself" when she was high or drunk than when she was sober. Weirdly, I think I knew what she was talking about. I remembered feeling like my party days served to get me out of my shell. Kelsey was looking for a confident and expressive voice with no inhibitions, and with drugs and alcohol she could step into it. Even her mother frequently had a hard time finding her voice in stressful situations.

A decade later, I am so grateful that Kelsey is happy and healthy and took charge of her own recovery. I try my best to honor everyone's path—even if it takes them down the dark and difficult path of drugs and addictions—but, man, it's a lot harder to honor it when it is your own kid!

And yet I am so grateful for the entire experience! Here are some of the things I remain grateful for:

- Her mother (my ex-wife) and I had to drive down to visit Kelsey once a week for six straight weeks. It was seven hours of driving roundtrip. And it was fine. We worked through and healed some old stuff together and rallied together to support Kelsey.
- I learned how to support my daughter by mostly just being with her and not saving her or rescuing her. I learned that sometimes presence and patience can win out in the end.
- I learned ever more deeply how to do my best and yet surrender at the same time and that, in the depths of surrender, there is a great peace.
- For a few years afterward, her mother and I taught some classes to a bunch of other parents who had kids with drug and alcohol problems (most of whom were every bit as full of denial as I had been). We shared our story openly, honestly, vulnerably, and with heartfelt tears.
- I was grateful to go to AA meetings where I could feel palpable love in the room and got to see my teenage daughter leading the way.
- I was so grateful to meet Carolyn Conger and so thankful that she gave me hope by sharing her experience with her niece, which taught me to be patient.

I share a lot of stories in this book that are of a spiritual nature—things that take place in dreams and visions and other states of consciousness. But I am also living this human life wherein I am also a dad and try to weave the wisdom I glean in dreams and visionary experiences into this human life. I'm grateful for all my spiritual experiences as well as for simply being a dad.

I love you, Kelsey!

61

"See You Soon, Frère Mystico"

It is December 2009. Over a period of nearly six months, Brugh had taken a sabbatical from teaching and traveled to Mount Kailash in Tibet. He would teach tirelessly day after day after day, hour after hour, seemingly without taking any time off, and then periodically, as he would he put it, "remove my teacher's mask," leave, and take a sabbatical. He always told his students that he did not know when or if he would return. When he did return from this most recent sabbatical, his students said he was on fire, brimming with new energy and new teachings from his many months in Tibet. Many of them encouraged me to rejoin my year-round study group and work with Brugh and others again.

But I was tired. I missed Brugh and my fellow travelers, but I had my hands full with life, my family, and some serious financial issues. I would have to catch up with Brugh again at some point down the road.

But I never got the chance. In 2009, Brugh was diagnosed with pancreatic cancer. This was the second time for him—he beat it the first time decades earlier. This time it moved swiftly.

Carolyn Conger posted this message on Facebook:

Brugh passed away this evening, 12-23-09 at 7:31 p.m. in peace. Earlier I had whispered in his ear, "See you soon, Frère Mystico," and he laughed.

So to you, his spiritual friends, I say, grieve well and celebrate his life all over the world in your unique ways. And live his teachings, all he has given you, and pass them on. Honor him by being Unconditional Love.

Carolyn

Carolyn also shared this dream and story at Brugh's memorial service:

"I'd like to tell you a dream that I had. Most of you know that Brugh's brother Bob and myself took care of Brugh for the four months he was ill. My dreams were very intense during that time. I had this dream that I call "THE RED SHOES" one month before Brugh died.

Brugh and I are walking towards a medical building – it is a huge building, like at UCLA or some other teaching hospital.

Brugh is walking in front of me (he always did—his legs are longer than mine) and I'm trotting behind. He always had a gait—he's charging ahead if there's something to do.

He has in his hands a leash with a little black dog on it and the dog is some kind of a long-haired shepherd. We are going into the medical building, and I'm struck by how large it is when we go in. We walk through many doors and finally get to the right place which is a doctor's office.

We enter the door of the doctor's office and right on the inside on the left is a kind of medical screen that's made of iron. It's curved and has little gathered curtains in it. Behind this screen, which is white, is a proper doctor in a white coat and stethoscope and all of that.

We take the dog—we are going inside the waiting room and go behind the screen and put the dog on the table to examine it and take care of it.

Brugh and I go back into the waiting room and the waiting room changes into something very beautiful. There are no chairs anymore and the room is very long. There are pools everywhere—beautiful natural pools in a nature setting and there are seven of them. There's also a light mist that is here.

Well, Brugh is delighted that we've gone into this arena, and he says, "Come on!" and he jumps into the first pool with his clothes on. "Come on Carolyn!" Well, I'm not as long legged as Brugh so I slide into the first pool and we are in there for a bit.

Pretty soon Brugh hops up and he says "OK, let's go to the next one!" We go on to the next one and I get in and get out. We go through all of the first six pools.

And then Brugh begins to get really excited—I mean the kind of excitement a five-year-old might get if he got a new Nintendo or Xbox. Jumping up and down. So excited. I'm still standing there at the side of the pool.

Brugh then runs over to another area on the right where there is a chest filled with people's shoes—such as outside a temple where you would leave your shoes. He reaches into this chest and pulls out a pair of women's red patent leather flats with a toe strap—they are shiny red— extraordinarily red. He then becomes very excited, jumping up and down, and he puts them on and says, "They fit!"

And then he runs and jumps into the seventh pool. The minute he does that and waves to me, the fog comes in very quickly.

I say to Brugh "I'm losing you."

She continued, "That dream is about me as much about Brugh. In interpreting the dream as Brugh's dream, I felt the dog being left behind represented Brugh's body being worked on. And the journey to the pools is his soul and my soul going through the motions of progressing in some way—from one pool to the next.

"It's his soul's choice to take the red shoes—which just like Dorothy's shoes—means going Home. Brugh always thought the feminine was soul energy. And the excitement and joy of that is what I want to remember.

"Even though we did all we could with so many wonderful physicians and helpers and anything you could have wanted for someone who was ill, his soul was choosing to go Home. I see it as a completion.

"It was a magnificent dream and it prepared me. Of course, I told it to Brugh—we shared all of our dreams. And in the beginning he asked me, 'Do you think it is a death dream?' And I said, 'Yes.' He said, 'Well I think it could also be something else. It could be the red shoes could be vitality coming in and a rebirth and the seventh pool could be the healing.'

"So right up to the end we were juggling these 2 different interpretations.

"It was a beautiful dream of mine that he honored and that was meaningful to me. He had me share the dream with several people to see their interpretations of it.

"But what I want to remember is that joyful, joyful feeling that he had of going Home—into the seventh pool.

"At some level he was prepared for death—we talked about it often. We still worked as if he would live—we worked very hard to keep him alive and yet he was prepared.

"And now his soul is knowing a lot of things that we don't know now."

A few days after Brugh's passing, Tom Kenyon shared this unexpected encounter with Brugh:

A Meeting with Brugh Joy

Note: I never met Brugh Joy in person although his writings had been a very influential force in my own work.

In the last few years of his life, we corresponded by email and had spoken once by phone. Brugh was an extraordinary person and a remarkable teacher.

Upon hearing about his death, from my friend Ken Ballard (a long-time student and friend of Brugh's), I entered into meditation to see if I might be of any assistance to Brugh as he traveled through the Bardos. I needn't have worried. I saw him as a meteor passing through the wrathful manifestations (one of the phases of the Bardos).

I did not give Brugh any further thought until a few days later, when he showed up unannounced in my mental world.

December 27, 2009

It happened around 3:00 a.m. after I had been working in my studio on a new a recording called "Manna." Suddenly, without any previous thought about him, I had a very strong impression of Brugh standing in front of me.

He was vividly clear in his luminous light body.

I asked him what it was like on the other side of the veil, and he chuckled. He said it was like taking off an old ill-fitting shoe. And then he said, it was much more than that. He was so very much aware of the many multiple dimensions of himself in ways he had not been aware of before.

He went on to say that he had become aware of himself as an almost infinitely faceted diamond, and that he could, if he chose, be aware of every facet simultaneously.

He then asked if he might give me something.

I said yes, and he handed me a coconut. As he passed it into my hands (all of this taking place in my mind's eye) the coconut began to sprout, and a green shoot broke through the hard husk of the shell. As this occurred, tears flowed from my eyes as I felt something within me opening.

The sprout quickly turned into a palm tree and suddenly I was on a beach in Guam where I had spent time as a child.

165

Brugh was now walking with me on the beach under a starlit sky.

We walked along the beach for some time in silence, me marveling at the peace of the moment and the vivid sense that this encounter with Brugh was real, even though it was taking place days after he had died.

Brugh then asked if he could show me something. As he said these words, he pointed off into the night sky to an area of pitch black between the luminous stars.

I said yes, to please continue.

"That is your shadow," he said, motioning to the dark portal. There was a twinkle of cosmic mischief in his eyes as he said these words. And then he looked straight into me.

"There is power out there, you know."

I nodded.

He then motioned to the dark patch of black in the sky. "Of course, out there is also in there." And with those words, he pointed to my chest.

"Life," he said, "is a dream with no beginning or ending. Enter the Mysterium and fly."

Those of us who were affected by Brugh's immense presence, no doubt, sense the loss. It is, therefore, a time for grieving. But it is also a time for celebration—to continue on with the Great Work.

"Enter the Mysterium and fly!"

Tom Kenyon

December 27, 2009

Carolyn Conger

Tom Kenyon

Brugh Joy

My heart swells with gratitude and love as I read these stories. I cry tears of humble and sincere appreciation for all that the three of you have so selflessly shared with me and with the rest of the world.

Thank you.

62

Live What You Don't
Want to Keep

In 2009 and 2010, a lot of things were happening at once—my daughter was in trouble with drugs and alcohol and shady friends, the recession was crushing my business and we were losing $20K per month, my wife was in fear about our financial situation and trying to protect her young girls from my wild teenagers, and I was feeling a gradual increase in lost passion. Ugh. Then, a voice came to me in a dream one night:

"Live what you don't want to keep."

I didn't want ANY of this! While I suppose I quite literally could have run away from my kids and my wife and my business and never return, I didn't choose to.

I chose to be here. I choose to be here. Even though it sometimes sucks.

So, the best option then is to embrace all of the difficulties and learn from them. To really LIVE all of this even though I would prefer to run away. I don't want to get stuck in a whiney victim place and instead want to try and embrace it. All of it.

If I do this, I can learn and grow.

In 2002, during an earlier difficult time, my doctor prescribed antidepressants. I took them for one week and then said, "Fuck it," and threw the rest of them away. That night, I lay awake all night shaking and sweating profusely. (I had no idea that giving up antidepressants after taking them for only one week could cause such powerful withdrawal symptoms.)

A year later, I gave up drinking. I stopped taking pain pills like Advil, Tylenol, and aspirin. I told myself I wanted to learn and grow and feel and experience *everything*—even if it was hard.

But I have my limits.

I got my wisdom teeth pulled in 2006 (all four were severely impacted so it was a difficult surgery), and afterward, the surgeon warned me to start taking Percocet *before* I started feeling any pain. But I liked being completely drug- and alcohol-free and thought I could just ride out the pain. But no. The pain was horrific. I took the Percocet.

But, in general, I've tried to embrace things I would rather run from. Instead, I've chosen to learn and grow from them, and try to experience them all directly.

It seems like we always have the choice to leave or stay in any situation we are in. But if we can't leave, or choose not to, it seems like the best way forward is to "live it" even if we don't really want to "keep it."

63

Bathtub Shadow Work

D r. William Brugh Joy sincerely asserted that all problems with others could be solved with heart-centering and shadow work; that by lovingly and compassionately acknowledging that the very thing you see in another person that pisses you off is in *you*, the trigger is unhooked; and that stepping into someone else's shoes and seeing what they see, hearing what they hear, and experiencing what they are experiencing is true compassion. Getting remarried and blending a family is often not easy, so I had plenty of opportunities to practice this.

It was 2009, and I was having a big argument with my wife. I thought her anger was way over the top—and not my fault at all. And then Brugh showed up that night in a dream:

> *I am wearing my wife's clothes—bright reddish-orange panties and a white sleeveless spaghetti-strap blouse. Brugh is wearing the same thing but with purple panties. We are in a bathroom and climb into the bathtub together. There is a table between us. I am eating dinner. Before I finish my meal, Brugh takes my plate away and says, "Now tell me about the crazed woman."*

Brugh seemed to walk his talk, and I think by having the dream wherein we were sitting in the tub together and both of us wearing my wife's clothing, he was trying to remind me that there is another choice besides anger and argument. Heart center. Take back projections. See the world through her eyes. Move to compassion—for me and for her. Go deep. See what is really going on. It's not out there!

It took years for me to really grok this, and I still have to remember and remind myself to do this. The instinct to get defensive and argumentative and to point fingers was an old and well-ingrained habit!

64

I Had a Dream There Were Two of Us!

At times, I have been a Tarot addict. I have over a dozen decks. I just love the visuals. I often put them all away for a few months, thinking I am done with the cards, but I always take them out again. I am still learning to love and appreciate and trust my own intuition, but the images in the Tarot are like a crutch I have a hard time giving up.

For the last two weeks, I have been working with The Mayan Oracle deck. It's one of my favorites. The last four times I randomly drew a card, I selected "Portal of Transcendence." The chances of selecting the same card four times in a row on four different days are extremely unlikely, so I paid attention.

This morning in meditation, I asked to go through this portal into transcendence. And I did. While in "transcendence," it felt like I was just hanging out in the void. Just hanging out. Hanging out. Very nice. Peaceful. There was no longer any me, just an infinite peace.

And then a voice erupts out of nowhere and excitedly yells, "I had a dream there were *TWO* of us!"

Instantly, I am overcome with bliss and ecstasy and thrown out of the void into temporality. End of meditation.

Hmmm . . .

All this time I had been seeking transcendence, unity, and eternity. And eternity thinks that nothing in this universe could possibly be as exciting as splitting into two and entering temporality! Duality yearns for nonduality. And perhaps nonduality yearns for duality!

65

Compassion for Leaders

It is 2010, and I'm having dreams and experiences that want to teach me that even the great leaders and famous spiritual teachers are still human. They are not always perfect. They too have doubts and fears and limitations. In one dream, I meet George Bush:

I am about to enter a charity race. George Bush is there to support the event. I walk up to him and warmly shake his hand. I feel such enormous compassion for him. He immediately opens up and starts telling me all about his personal life. He says it is so hard living with four sisters. He says he has slept with each one of them (I don't think he means sexually—I think he means he has spent the night and knows each one well). His eyes are full of tears, and he is stammering and looking away. I can feel grief, guilt, and pain for lives lost in Iraq. I have so much to ask him about what it is like to be in his skin, but I say nothing. I simply hold him in a safe healing container of unconditional love. He stammers on and on about more personal stuff and releases so much baggage.

During my study with Brugh, I recalled him saying that the most projected upon person in the entire world is the president of the United States and that to most people he is either an angel/savior or a devil. I didn't like Bush then, but the dream shifted everything for me. It was the very beginning of compassion in me for both leaders and for myself. I had standards that perhaps were a bit too high. I liked to revere great leaders and put them on a pedestal, and if they behaved in a way that I perceived as being out of integrity, I would swiftly knock them off their pedestal and move on.

In another dream, I again met Adi Da Samraj—"the Avataric Incarnation of Conscious Light." He came to my house with head bowed. He had some humbling relationship issues he needed help with. The great Adi Da—the Divine Giver—was having some very real human problems and wanted my help.

I also met Barack Obama in a dream. While we hung out, he shared his fears and uncertainties about being president with me. He said that he wasn't always sure what the right course of action was, that he was embarrassed he had not been able to quit smoking. I just hung out and listened to him pour out his anxieties.

Compassion. Even for the great leaders. Even for myself. This was a difficult lesson for me.

66

The Dalai Lama Makes a House Call

This story came from a dream I had in 2010:

Last night the Dalai Lama dropped by my house. He arrived wearing his crimson robes and said he'd heard I was not sleeping well and struggling with anxiety.

This was true.

He asked me to stand and then performed some sort of healing ritual on me. Afterward, I did feel a bit more peaceful. But my new peace was sort of drowned out by my shock that the Dalai Lama had made a house call!

He did seem to be in a bit of a hurry and began to change his clothes right in front of me. Sheez . . . he was so . . . small. Skinny. Pale. Bald. Without his glasses or his crimson robes, I didn't even recognize him.

In a weird way, he was now no longer the Dalai Lama. In fact, he very casually says, "My name is Tenzin Gyatso," like he was just a regular Joe introducing himself. And in an instant, it was like we were brothers, best friends, with nothing to hide. Just me and him.

Tenzin gets dressed in street clothes. I bend over and give him a hug and begin to softly sob on his tiny, little shoulders.

I forget that so many of the "greats"—presidents, prime ministers, CEOs, spiritual teachers, etc. seemingly so different, so aloof, and so "great" are also just people, so human, and that, well, we also share a lot in common.

My new buddy Tenzin had to run, but maybe if he had some more time we could have jumped in the car and gone on a road trip and maybe just hung out together. I would have liked that.

67

My Little Angel

It is around 5:00 p.m., and I decide to meditate for a short spell before my wife and I leave for our dinner reservation. A vexing problem has been bugging me, and I think that meditating might give me a break from fretting about it so much.

I am not into the meditation for even five minutes when I see a tiny angel made entirely of light leave the center of my body, shoot out the top of my head, and plunge upward into what looks like a white star right above my head. I see it gather a bunch of light and dive right back down into my head, and I can feel the tiny angel of light slowly go down through each of my chakras and exit my root.

Start to finish, the whole thing took all of ten seconds, and my vexing problem is solved in the process! Plus, I feel so vital and alive. Jeez . . . like I got an electrifying jolt of happy caffeine! I also feel a weird sense of extreme clarity, like for a short time, I can calmly and knowledgeably speak about anything! I am enlivened and illumined.

I recall my brother had a funny quirk when he was young where, when he needed an answer, he would roll his eyeballs upward as if searching for the answer "up there" somewhere in his brain. Maybe the answers *are* up there—but above and beyond our brains. Maybe we all have tiny angels of light within us who go out and get information for us from a star above us, and maybe our brains are processors that try to make sense of all the information our own tiny angels of light deliver to us.

68

Moving from Blue to Red

I t is 2010, and I hear a voice that says:

"The entire world is moving from blue to red."

And as the decade progressed, it definitely did. If politically the color red represents patriarchal nationalism, fundamentalism, and authoritarianism, the world most definitely did move from blue to red.

But why?

If the forces of chaos and great change run amok—maybe there is too much change in a short period of time—do the forces of fundamentalism, order, and control rise up to keep it in check?

I have wondered if the swift changes brought on by technology and the immense uncertainty in job markets have created underlying collective anxiety and fear. There has been a massive increase in shared information via the internet, social media, and exposure to darn near everything in TV and movies, not to mention fake news everywhere. Things that not so long ago were forbidden—abortion, gay marriage, and countless other issues—are front and center. Maybe all that change is happening too quickly. Maybe too much change all at once creates fear, and when fear pervades the populace, "they" look for an authoritarian father figure to give them a sense of safety and ask him to reestablish what feels like order and control.

Maybe the reverse is true as well: When there is too much safety, order, and control, the world begins to feel bored and stifled and becomes thirsty for change and thus turns blue again.

69

Wise Elephant

I am participating in a Warrior Weekend with an organization called the ManKind Project in November 2011.

I am doing a journey to find my animal totem. Immediately, in my mind's eye, I see a black jaguar. From the outset of my spiritual quest, this big black cat has been my totem.

I love cats and especially big black jaguars. In the Mayan tradition, the black jaguar is *Ix* (pronounced *eesh*) and is associated with seeing in and being fearless of the dark. For nearly ten years now, I have been using the heart center and unconditional love to interiorly and exteriorly bravely explore all the things that scare me.

But as I am riding on the back of my big black jaguar under a full moon deep into the jungle, I see a lone male elephant up ahead. And my jaguar takes me and puts me on the back of the elephant, and a new animal name/totem is born.

I am no longer Black Jaguar.

I am now Wise Elephant.

I come out of the journey shocked, surprised, and overjoyed. I knew somehow that this handoff from Black Jaguar to Wise Elephant was significant.

I did not know it at the time, but this was the last time I would ever see a black jaguar in my dreams and visions. It heralded the end of choosing to go *into* the dark, the frightening, and the scary, and instead was a movement into wisdom, elderhood, and the adoption of a new identity as an "old soul."

I'd had what felt like entire lifetimes full of expansion, growth, and many varied experiences, and now it was time to slow down and weave everything into my life and try to live it. To ground and integrate. And to share it.

70

Jungle Initiation and Transcendence

It is 2012, and I am having a dream . . .

I am on the back of an elephant who takes me deep into the jungle at midnight. There is a large circular clearing in the middle of the dense jungle. A full moon is illuminating the clearing. I climb off the elephant and stand in the center of the clearing.

Surrounding me are what look like nearly one hundred native tribesmen all wearing black-and-white-striped T-shirts. All at once, they begin throwing heavy metal spears at me. Their spears tear through my flesh, but curiously, they do not hurt me.

Suddenly, with my body full of spears, I begin to grow and grow and grow. Soon I am as tall as the trees and then bigger than the mountains, and then all the spears fall away like so many tiny toothpicks.

Soon, I am as big as the universe itself, and the drama taking place in the jungle on planet Earth is very small indeed.

71

Immanent and Transcendent

I am meditating in the quiet of the early morning. I feel like I am in my heart center, and I am peacefully aware of my breath. Really nice.

Something brand new is happening.

I sense what feels like light, deep inside my chest, sending a wave of love through my body out to my aura, the energetic field surrounding my body. Then the energy field sends a wave of love back to the light deep inside my chest.

I can't see this. I only feel it. There is a love affair going on between what I perceive to be the light inside me and the light that surrounds me.

It is subtle but indescribably beautiful. Back and forth it goes. A warm wave of love is sent out. It moves achingly slow. Maybe ten seconds goes by, and then a slow, warm wave of love is sent back in. Over and over and over this goes on, back and forth, back and forth, back and forth.

What is this? Even as I am enjoying feeling these slow, warm waves of love being sent back and forth, my mind, as always, is trying to explain it.

I know people who say God is inside of them (God is immanent) and those who say God is outside them (God is transcendent). Maybe both are true, and in my quiet and peace, I was graced with feeling God share this great love—where the One became two and the two realizing and recognizing they are One.

72

Scorpios and Scorpions

I have a newfound interest in astrology. I'm at my friend Cassandra's house in Fresno, California. It's only the second time we have met in person. We are longtime Facebook and email friends, plus over the last five years we shared a lot of dreams on a dream forum.

She suggested we both get astrology readings and share them with each other during my visit. She told me she is a Scorpio and that a lot of other parts of her astrological chart were in Scorpio. I had learned a bit about Scorpio and the dark feminine, as well as why the scorpion was the symbol for this sign. Symbolically, the scorpion kills the "old you" so that a "new you" can be born. According to my astrologer, I was going through an intense Pluto transit, and that this sort of transformation was up for me now.

I arrived there in the evening, and Cassandra suggested that when we get up in the morning, we share our astrology readings over breakfast. I had the high points of my astrology reading all typed up into about four pages of bullet points. The pages were on the floor next to my bed.

When I get up in the morning and I go to get my pages, I am dismayed to see a bug is smashed on one of the pages. It sort of smeared the line that read, "Scorpio is very active in your life now." When I look closer, I am surprised to see that the smashed bug is actually a small scorpion!

What are the chances that a scorpion (symbol of Scorpio) gets crushed on the second page of an astrology reading exactly on the line that talks about how active Pluto (ruler of Scorpio) is in my chart in the home of someone who is a Scorpio and who carries lots of Scorpio energy?

Cassandra's reaction? "Oh yeah, that kinda stuff happens to me all the time."

73

Ketu

I am meditating.

It's 2012, and for the past three or four years, I have been feeling a lot of what feels like emptiness. Although, that isn't entirely accurate. More accurately, it felt like my bucket list of things I wanted to do as well as things I used to like to do were drying up. Having been an action-oriented and passionate guy for my entire life, this was all disconcerting.

Nearly every day felt a lot like the movie *Groundhog Day*. I kept waiting and seeking something new to excite me—a new hobby, interest, or passion—but nothing was forthcoming. "I don't care" became my mantra.

I had learned to trust in the spiritual journey, but there were nagging voices saying that maybe I had a physical issue. Did I need an antidepressant?

But if I sat still and looked within, I knew that I was not depressed. I heard someone say the word *dispassion* once and I thought *that* was it. But are there medical or pharmaceutical cures for dispassion?

Anyway . . . I am meditating. Even my meditations had become about as interesting as driving to work. Ugh.

"I can't get no . . . satisfaction."

Anyway, yeah, sigh . . . I am meditating.

And then an elderly Asian woman pops into my meditation and says, *"John, you are a high Ketu."*

Well, this ended my sense of bored emptiness. Who was this woman and what did she mean? Prior to this, I had not heard of Ketu. In fact, since it was spoken to me, I didn't even know how to spell it.

K2? Was she referring to the mountain? I am a high mountain?

I tried to spell it phonetically. KATU? I looked it up and kept getting things like "Radio station KATU!"

I was striking out when Google asked if I was looking for "Ketu." So, I clicked on it and found a bunch of sites all about Ketu! Here is a general summary:

KETU: From Vedic astrology, Ketu is symbolized by a headless serpent or a headless dragon who is forever looking for his lost desire. Someone under the influence of Ketu is often in a chronic state of restlessness, discontent, and dissatisfaction. Ketu works with Ganesh, the remover of obstacles, to remove all attachments—both positive and negative. Its goal is to move one away from typical human passions and to radically cut away everything that no longer serves. It is auspicious if one is seeking enlightenment but malefic for nearly everything else. The best way to move through a Ketu cycle is to surrender all judgments and expectations.

It is hard to put into words how happy this made me. All this emptiness and restless discontent . . . I wasn't making it all up. I didn't need to go see a doctor.

I had never heard of Ketu prior to this and didn't know there was such a thing as Vedic astrology. But just to confirm everything, I found a Vedic astrologer nearby and made an appointment to meet with him.

When I met Dennis about a week later, he humorously said that while he gets clients from many walks of life, this was the first time he got a new client from a dream! For the next hour he proceeded to teach me all about the influence of Ketu in my astrological chart and what it was trying to accomplish.

Weirdly, this was one of the most important experiences of my life. My trust in the unfolding of my life grew tremendously, and I learned that even when *nothing* is happening, that *something* is happening. I admit that I still prefer at least some degree of desire and passion and intensity, but I am learning to see and experience life in different ways as well. I have learned to trust the not knowing and, wherever I can, to let go of all expectations.

Apparently, this is not an unusual experience, and many people are affected by the emptying influence of Ketu. Good to know when occasionally seeing people wandering around, looking for their lost desires.

74

Wisdom Wine

I am a bright red Zinfandel.
Zesty.
Full of life.
Such a plump cluster I was.
Plucked lovingly and hauled off to a place I'd never been.
Then crushed.
My skins stripped away.
Only my sweet juice, my essence, remained.
Blended with other grapes.
And then I sat in the dark.
Days, weeks, months.
Transformation.
In an old oak barrel.
Then light.
Blinding. Intense.
Poured into a sleek and curvy clear bottle.
With a sexy label.
Corked.
And shipped to Seattle.

Displayed.
My fiery, zesty, red essence.
To be shared selflessly with another.
But it's not my time yet.
I sit in a dark, damp, cool, musty cellar.
I am impatient with all the stillness and darkness.
But I will mature.
My flavors will marry.
My zesty power will mellow
Into something smoother, more complex.
And yet simpler.
That is easy
And a joy to consume.

75

Satya (Truth)

I took a short nap yesterday, and in the middle of a dream, a loud voice proclaimed, "TRUTH BE TOLD!" and it woke me up. So, I wrote it down and began to muse about truth.

Jeez . . . is there a word more used and misused, understood and misunderstood in the world today than *truth*?

Recently, I had a profound dream while meditating . . .

I see myself leave Earth as if in a rocket ship, and I blast off at high speed. As I pass through the blue haze/atmosphere that surrounds our planet, a voice tells me that contained within this blue band are archetypes. As I continue higher and farther, I pass stars and planets and a whole lot of black space. And then, as if I were that character in The Truman Show, *I leave the show and exit the space with all its darkness and stars and planets and archetypes, and I enter a realm of infinite, clear light. A goddess appears and tells me her name is Satya. Satya implores me, "OPEN! OPEN! OPEN!" and shows me an image of a red rosebud opening.*

To this day, this dream has had a profound impact on me. Somehow it seemed to be telling me that beyond our world of archetypes, planets, and stars, dark and light lies an infinite realm of light. As if maybe the play of light and dark is somehow held or enclosed by infinite light. *Satya. Truth.* Is this the real truth? The ultimate truth? Somehow, *Satya* wanted me to open to this.

So, what *is* truth? Is our human understanding of truth like a stairway of understanding where at each step we see and perceive truth differently?

Mahatma Gandhi spoke eloquently about truth and called it a powerful force—far more powerful than lies or falsehoods. In fact, the alternate title of his autobiography is *The Story of My Experiments with Truth*. Truth here is a force.

In politics, "truth" seems to be whatever one side or the other wants it to be. The truth is endlessly spun and twisted and manipulated in an effort to convince and manipulate others. Truth in politics is something to manipulate and wield for power and control and for winning and losing.

In astrology, my Sun sign is in Sagittarius, and it is said that Sagittariuses love the truth. In fact, they have been accused of being a bit too truthful at times. Sag's just spit it out and call it as they see it. Truth here is what I see.

In science, truth might be a majority consensus wherein, if a large majority objectively agree on something, then it is proclaimed as truth. Truth here is what smart people who agree say it is. To others, truth is what their group, tribe, church, or culture proclaims it to be, and others who are a part of that group/tribe willingly agree. Truth here is what a likeminded group decides it is.

Mavericks and others who have no interest in tribal groupthink may proclaim their own truth. Only their own individual truth matters.

Edgar Cayce, a great Christian prophet, and the Godfather of holistic medicine was able to access truth (all events that ever took place anywhere and everywhere by anyone in the past) in service to others. Truth to Cayce was exactly what happened prior to any personal mental or emotional manipulation of the facts.

In *A Course in Miracles*, a popular course with 365 daily lessons taught over a full year, truth is what lies beyond the ego. Speaking from one's core or center would be truth, and all else is not truth. Truth here is more like essence or divinity.

Adyashanti (Adya) said that lashing out at others in anger—"I hate you and you ruined my life!"—is how we hide from the truth. To Adya, truth was something far deeper than our emotional outbursts.

For some, the entire spiritual journey is a quest for truth and deep-felt yearning for truth. It may begin with a deep, heartfelt desire for honesty and authenticity. To be honest with oneself. To be honest with others. To be in the company of others who are equally honest and authentic. Groupthink, consensus, and manipulation simply become less interesting.

But maybe that is just the beginning of the quest.

Maybe after one has realized their own honesty and authenticity and are standing on their own two feet beyond groupthink, consensus, and manipulation, they still yearn for something more, and they search for an even greater truth.

More than one spiritual teacher has proclaimed that the path to God/Oneness/Spirit begins with *knowing about* God/Oneness/Spirit—through church, family, books, scripture, news, science, dreams, and revelations—and then one begins to surrender all that great heap of accumulated knowledge and one is then dissolved into God/Oneness/Spirit. One then learns about God/Oneness/Spirit by *becoming* it!

Maybe this is the same for truth. Perhaps one learns all about truth—what is true, what is false, what is honesty, and what is a lie—and before one can help others see and realize truth, one must first swim in the muck of manipulating truth and being manipulated by falsehoods. And then, one day, one is no longer all that interested in truth or falsehood, news or fake news, and instead one simply *becomes* the truth. Perhaps one's core identity and core truth simply go from "I am a human being" to "I am the infinite." And *becoming the truth* starts to be simply what is and is experienced like flow or synchronicity.

Maybe this is the strata of truth, the spectrum of truth, and the ladder we all must climb if the yearning for truth compels us. Ever since I had that dang dream, it's been pushing me, compelling me, and urging me on.

I feel a great affection for Satya.

Truth.

76

Buddha in My Car

I'm driving to work. It's a dreary day in winter of 2013. It's rush hour. I am getting close to work, but I am stopped now in a long line of cars at a red light. It is a typical cold and gray, damp Seattle morning. I am feeling mopey and empty. Dispassionate. Bored. I don't care.

While sitting there dejectedly, a profound, booming, deep voice, coming up from the bowels of the Earth that feels like it belongs to the Buddha, speaks through my body and says:

"Can't you see that on the other side of 'I don't care' is complete freedom?! BWAHAHAHAHA!"

Grinding. One by one all the things I used to love and care about were ground down to dust. I went from being passionate and caring to being dispassionate and not caring about much at all. The passion was ground down and ground down, and the bucket list was emptied. There remained just a present equanimity that felt like emptiness. Nothingness. That I fought and fought and fought. And fought some more. Passion and caring were of infinitely more value than not caring or emptiness or dispassion. Or so I thought.

But after all the grinding and emptying, I just began to give in. Surrender. Let go.

And what I found in its place was not "nothing" nor "I don't care" but a deep love and acceptance and reverence for *everything*. For life. All of it. For the white sheep *and* the black sheep. Both.

So today it's not so much "I love this (but not that)." Or "I care for this (but not that)." There's just love. And there is more universal care for *everything*, not just my personal and very selective cares.

The grinding toward what still sometimes feels like emptiness continues to this day. I still fight it. But I don't fight it as much. I can feel the immense love behind everything. Letting go, letting go some more, and letting go ever deeper.

77

Cutthroat

This is a fictional story I wrote in 2014 wherein I tried to capture what happens when someone is given inner guidance, follows it, and experiences a heartfelt sense of gratitude and appreciation for that guidance:

It was a hot August afternoon when I drove north to fish a secret stretch of the Stillaguamish River. When I arrived at the river, I saw that it was flowing low and clear. Just a lazy, languid ribbon of blue water slipping gracefully through the evergreens and broad farming valley.

As fall was near, salmon were beginning to poke their noses in the river. The sea-run cutthroat trout would be right there with them. Summer run steelhead were in the river too but probably far upstream. Today I was fishing a long, lazy estuary near the mouth of the river.

I knotted a pale-yellow Knudsen Spider fly onto my tippet. It was a fly that sea-runs were often fond of, though occasionally the early running pinks and king salmon would make a pass at it.

It was easy fishing—long casts made to overhanging brush and tangled logs. Both the salmon and the sea-runs would be hiding out in the slow, deep water with lots of dark cover while they made their way upstream

It was nearly the bewitching hour. That magical time as the sun begins to set and the shadows lengthen. I had barely begun fishing when I had my first take. It was a solid jolt as the fly swung through the deep shadowy pool at the base of a steep ledge piled high with flood debris, logs, and rocks.

The fish was large and fought stubbornly deep in the shadows. And then it just gave up. It swam right to my feet where it lay gasping in the shallows.

It was a fine, large, male sea-run cutthroat. Fresh from the sea, it was covered in many tiny black spots on a gleaming silver body. Two sea lice were still present, indicating it had only recently entered the river.

With fly rod held high, I gently scooped up the fish with my left hand and held it next to the ruler markings on my rod. It was a full eighteen inches long. Two beautiful, bright-orange slashes on his throat were the telltale sign that this was a sea-run cutthroat. I gently removed the barbless hook from his lower jaw. I paused and admired his beauty and fresh, wild, clean lines and sharp fins and tail. His eyes were focused and magnificent—like an underwater eagle.

He had given me all I wanted of him, so I lowered him to the water to gently release him. After all, like the salmon, he was on a journey home to the waters of his birth to spawn.

But as he touched the water, he sat bolt upright in my hands and said, "STOP!"

"Did you just say, 'Stop'?" I inquired.

"Yes! You're not supposed to let me go. That's not how the dream goes."

"What am I supposed to do?"

"You're supposed to kill me and eat me."

"Well, I no longer kill fish. I am a catch-and-release fisherman. Besides, you are on your spawning journey."

"Yeah, well, I've done that before. A couple of times. We're not like the salmon. We can spawn every year—if we survive. But my journey this time ends with you."

"I'd rather not kill you. I just like to come down here for peace and quiet. The fishing is something I do to take my mind off my harried life. I admire your strength and beauty but have no desire to kill you and eat you."

"But the dream says you must. It is time."

"What dream? Do fish have dreams?"

"I do. And this dream is very clear and has been appearing night after night. My journey ends here. You kill me and eat me."

"Well, if this is your last day here on Earth, and since we are having this fine conversation, can you tell me about yourself? Where were you born? What is it like being a fish? What is it like being a sea-run cutthroat?"

"Thank you so much for asking! Well, I was born in a tiny tributary to this great river called St. Francis Creek. My brothers, sisters, and I all hatched about four years ago. But the tiny creek had very little food in it and often flowed swiftly. So, we drifted downstream to a pretty little beaver pond where we lived for a full year, growing fat on tadpoles, dragonflies, damselflies, mosquitoes, mayflies, and more. It was a perfect little nursery. It was an old pond with lots of brush. The brush kept us safe from herons and raccoons.

"I loved that old pond. It was on the property of a young couple who were always outside and hanging around the pond. I would see them feeding the birds—there were a LOT of birds there! They were not your usual Dead People. No, they were alive and connected to the land in a rare way. He was always talking to the birds. The rabbits would follow him everywhere. She would speak lovingly to the raspberries as she plucked them off the vines. In the fall, they would remove some of the woody debris to clear the inlet and outlet of the old pond so the salmon and the spawning sea-run cutthroat could make it home to spawn. They all passed through the old pond coming and going—from sea to home and from home to sea.

"In my second year, my brothers and sisters and I answered the yearning to leave our little nursery pond and ride the heavy spring floodwater down St. Francis Creek to this great river. We were all so excited and so scared!

"But the great river was a dark, muddy torrent and not at all like our little nursery pond. There was almost no food. There were thousands, maybe millions of baby salmon, cutthroat, and steelhead all fighting for our lives in the unfriendly and powerful dark river.

"My brothers and sisters and I were well fed and healthy from growing up in our little pond, and we survived the journey to the sea. But we were greeted by predators of all sorts—adult salmon, big sea-runs, seals, otters, raccoons, herons, and eagles all waited to pick us off as we entered the sea, weak and disoriented. I lost many of my brothers and sisters the first few days after we hit the sea.

"But about ten of us made it. We didn't travel all the way to Alaska like the salmon and the steelhead. No, we stayed pretty close to home. We would cruise the estuary and swim up and down the beach for a few miles or so.

"The sea was bountiful and good to us. We ate shrimp, sand lance, and herring, and quickly grew very healthy and fat. We stayed in the shallows away from all the big predators. It wasn't as safe as our nursery pond, but it was generous, and we learned to love life in the sea.

"Late in the summer of the following year, I felt the changes in my body and the call to return to St. Francis Creek. It was an amazing time of year. Millions upon millions of salmon—now very BIG—were returning home as well. My brothers and sisters and I followed the salmon into the rivers of our birth and headed upstream.

"It did not take long before I could smell my beautiful St. Francis Creek. I took a right turn and, after a mile or so, was back in my beloved pond. The little fish there gave me a wide berth as I was a full twelve inches long now. But I had other things on my mind besides eating. I followed the tiny inlet to the pond up to a shallow stretch of fine gravel and recognized the gravel as the stones of my birth.

"There were many fine females all heavily laden with eggs, but I had to prove my merit in battle before settling down with a mate.

Many sea-runs were far larger than I, but I was fierce. I tore at the fins and tails of many larger males. We all nearly killed each other, but soon we settled in, and each found our mates. Mine was a precious little female who powerfully scooped out a tiny nest and quickly deposited hundreds of precious little orange eggs in the shallow depression. I settled in close over the glowing embers and deposited my white seed. With powerful sweeping motions of her body, she then quickly covered the nest with fine gravel.

"Afterward, spent and weary, feeling barely alive, I drifted down to my little nursery pond and spent time recovering there. Many of my brothers and sisters did not make it. I sat still in that pond, eating very little and mostly just resting and recovering.

"When spring came, I headed back down St. Francis Creek to the great river and again followed it down to the sea. I was still weak and hungry, but the sea's bounty soon nursed me back to health. Most of my brothers and sisters were gone, but I made friends with new sea-runs. They became like brothers and sisters to me.

"That fall I, again, followed the salmon upstream and again, headed for upper St. Francis Creek—now a fine, strong fifteen-inch fish. Again, I battled for the hen of my desires, and again, while severely weakened by battle and little food, I survived to spawn yet again.

"It was early this year that I made it back to sea, and as you can see, I am a large, strong sea-run cutthroat. I thought I was going to go through the joys and rigors of spawning again, but life had a different plan for me. So here I am."

"Thank you so much for that story," I said. "I really appreciate it. So, does the dream tell you that I kill you now?"

"Yes."

"Does the dream tell me *how* I kill you?"

"Yes. You knock me out by striking my head firmly with a large rock and then you slit my throat."

"And then I take you home and eat you?"

"Yes. But the dream has asked me to tell you that you have two tasks—in addition to killing me and eating me."

"And they are?"

"After you slit my throat, please pause and hold me up to the light. You'll have to do this quickly as the sun will soon set. There will be something you must see."

"OK. And the second task?"

"When you have cooked me and get ready to eat me, please pause to remember me. I have been asked to offer my life to you."

"I will do this."

"Thank you, John."

"By the way, how is it that we can talk and how do you know my name?"

"I'm not really sure, but I think it's sort of like twin brothers. They often don't have to say anything at all to each other. They just know. Their hearts and minds are one. I think we're like that."

"Thank you."

"Know this, John: I am not afraid. You need to do this now. I've already been out of the water way too long and will not survive if you try to release me. And you must kill me before the sun goes down. Now. Please, you must kill me!"

With that, I picked up a smooth piece of river rock the size of my fist and cracked the sea-run's skull with three short, hard whacks. The sea-run cutthroat's eyes rolled into the center of their sockets.

And I reached into my vest for my pocketknife and slit the sea-run's throat. A rivulet of blood trickled down his silvery sides.

With the sea-run dead, his throat slit, and his head folded back, I held the fish up high above my head. The last remaining rays of sunlight shimmered across the estuarine meadows and the sharp, wild sea-run cutthroat trout—a mix of gleaming silver, black spots, sharp fins, orange slashes, and trickling blood—glowed in the fading light.

And then I felt a quaking in me.

A surge of ecstatic energy moved up through me, entering my feet and exiting my head and upstretched hands. I looked down and saw that I was standing on the lips of a beautiful woman with green hair and green eyes. She blew a kiss upward through my body. Then I felt a more subtle giddy energy move from my head down to my feet. I looked up, and a giant ancient man was kissing me lightly on the top of my head.

Standing between the kiss from both above and below and quaking in the final sunny rays of a late-August summer evening, I knew that I had somehow been graced.

That evening, mindful of my final task, I lovingly prepared my sea-run cutthroat trout for dinner. I prepared it simply—fresh bread crumbs, a little olive oil, and some salt and pepper.

I set the fish on the table, still steaming, and smelling wondrous. I clasped my hands, closed my eyes, and gave thanks.

78

Another Choice

Tramping over a bridge
Leaving the old
Crossing into the new
Paradise awaits
But for just a moment
I straddle two worlds
Neither leaving the old
Nor settling into the new
Perhaps there is another choice
Beneath my feet, a river joyously flows onward
Through crashing rapids and sacred pools
And occasionally flowing under big, old, shadowy bridges

79

No More Expectations

It is 2014, and Shonagh and I have been divorced for about two years, but we have been living in the same house. The 2008 recession caught up to us in 2009 and 2010 and put our home underwater. We couldn't afford to get divorced and live separately. Plus, my business was suffering, and we were barely staying afloat financially.

Back in 2008, I started to lose passion—not just physical passion but passion for everything. Most of the things I loved to do had up and disappeared. Money became tight, the roof had leaks, and the kitchen floor was warped. Blending a family had been hard, and it was clear as time went on that Shonagh and I were on two ships headed in different directions. So, in 2012, we got a divorce. There were no harsh words, and we worked together very well on behalf of each other and our children.

Over these past two years, things got better between us. It is like some veil of unconscious expectations has been lifted, and we aren't holding each other to those expectations anymore. She can be Shonagh, and I can be John. Still broke. Still living together. Still doing all the same things. But somehow it is all better. Somehow, we are free.

I wonder if part of the burden and difficulty in relationships and marriages are the expectations we have of our partners, and that these expectations might be entirely unconscious. A therapist told me once that after we sign the marriage contract, there is also an unknown and unconscious contract each partner brings to a relationship. For example, she said, a woman might marry a man for love, but unconsciously she also expects him to make her feel safe. If she feels unsafe, to her, he broke the contract.

If Shonagh and I did have unconscious contracts with each other, we are no longer bound by them. She is a force of will and a determined manifestor, and she has been holding the expectation of finding a small cottage to rent on a large piece of property. Frankly, I don't see anything like that in our area, and I am certain that anything on a large piece of property will be way too expensive, so I am not as "sure" as she is that it will happen.

But it does. She finds the perfect little cottage rental on fifteen acres of property, and it is walking distance to the girls' school. I am stunned. It is exactly what she had been looking for. The rent is reasonable, and we can make it happen.

She and the girls are in the cottage now, and I go over there about once a week to hang out and have dinner and catch up on things. I feel blessed by the ten years we all had together, and I am sad it ended. Yet I am also grateful for the ending and the new beginning.

I love you Shonagh, Maddie, and Serena!

80

Don't Worry, Be Happy

My consumer products company makes a wide variety of branded pet and household cleaning products sold in all large national retailers. It's 2014, and I am booked to fly on a business trip from Seattle to Jacksonville, Florida, with a connection in Dallas, and plans to fly back the same way the next day. It is a lot of flying for a thirty-minute sales presentation, but such is the nature of my business. I make about twenty of these trips a year.

On the day before I am to leave, I pull a muscle in my lower back. Crap.

I know how this will go. I have pulled a muscle in my lower back many times, and the thing that always made it worse was sitting for long periods of time. Walking and gentle stretching were helpful. Sitting was not.

Driving for long distances with my back thrown out has always been hell. Sitting for hours in an airplane will be even worse. I wonder if I will even be able to get out of my airplane seat and stand up by the time my first flight arrives in Dallas. There have been times over the years that my back was in so much pain that I used to have to grab the roof of my car with my hands and pull myself up just to get my legs out of the car. Most likely, it will take months for my back to fully heal.

The next morning, I wake up hoping for a miracle. No dice. My back is stiff and painful. I drive to the airport, and by the time I arrive, my pain and discomfort is at a six (out of ten). I am certain it will be a nine by the time I get to Florida. All told, it is three and a half hours of flying to Dallas, a one-hour layover, and then another two-and-a-half-hour flight to Jacksonville. Plus, a rental car drive to my hotel. Then sitting for dinner with my sales team, sitting in my presentation the next morning, and then doing it all over the next day on my return to Seattle. That's a whole lotta sitting.

Crap.

I try to keep my cool and just steel myself against the pain and for what will most certainly be more pain. I must get through the next thirty-six hours, and then I can start rehab when I get home.

As I am standing in line in security still grumbling to myself about how badly my back hurts and how much worse it will be by the end of the day, I suddenly become aware that some other aspect of "me" is quietly humming the song, "Don't Worry, Be Happy" and aiming the vibrations of this happy tune at my injured lower back. I don't know how this is happening. I just become aware of it. I, as I know myself to be, am not doing this. But it most certainly is happening.

Mind you, there are hundreds of people all around me here in the TSA-precheck line and I'm having this unexpected crazy internal experience. There's the "me" who is clearly angry and in his absolute tunnel-vision certainty that this was bad and would only get worse. But there was this other aspect that was peacefully and happily humming the upbeat song and seemed only interested in healing my back.

I decided to go with the singer and the song. I joined in and started humming, "Don't Worry, Be Happy" to my lower back. I was casually aware that energy and vibration could be healing. What did I have to lose?

I arrived and settled into my window seat, and my back was still stiff and sore. But I was immensely grateful for the distraction of humming the song and cautiously hoping that somehow it would make the trip more bearable.

I'm watching all the passengers coming down the aisle and am crestfallen when I see what looks like a sumo wrestler sit in the middle seat next to me. All the way to Dallas, I must sit pushed toward the window and with no armrest on my left side. Again, the grumbling voice said that my back would be even worse because I could not sit perfectly erect. In the past, sitting crooked was even worse than just plain sitting and always made my back pain worse. But I kept on humming. Over and over. Aiming the song at my lower back. I'm not self-conscious about this because the nice thing about all the ambient airplane noise is that no one can hear me humming.

When I arrive in Dallas, I am unusually happy. My pain has gone from a six to a four. This has never happened following an extended period of sitting with my back thrown out in an uncomfortable posture. The happy humming has not only helped with my back; it has perked up and erased my dour mood.

On the next flight, the same thing happens. An unusually large woman pins me against the window in an uncomfortable crooked posture, but I continue to hum, and by the time we deplane in Jacksonville, I am at a pain level of three. I hum to my back on the ride to the hotel. I quietly hum to myself over dinner with my two salesmen while they chatter away. I hum in my hotel room while getting ready for bed.

In the morning, my back is still stiff and sore but way better than the previous morning. I hum to myself over breakfast.

After our presentation, I hum on the way to the Jacksonville airport. I hum on the flight to Dallas even though yet again I am pinned next to the window by another very large man. I've been sitting in window seats while flying for decades and never encountered so many unusually large passengers sitting next to me in the middle seat.

But I'm gaining confidence in this new experience. I have this little Mona Lisa smile on my face wherein I am having this secret inner experience. I love that I am having this private experiment amidst all the chaos of travel.

As I board my final flight from Dallas to Seattle, I am happy. My pain is maybe a two. Just as it looks like we are about to leave our gate, I am elated to see I have an empty seat next to me. But I celebrated just a few seconds too soon.

A young woman is coming down the aisle toward the empty seat next to me with a young boy in her arms. I knew that it was OK for mothers to hold their children in their laps if the child was under age two. They both sit in the empty middle seat. The boy is sharing his mother's seat. To me he looks more like a three- or four-year-old, and his big feet with big shoes kick me over and over. I am once again pressed against the window.

No big deal. I hum, "Don't Worry, Be Happy," to myself again and again. It is a long four-plus-hour flight.

My Mona Lisa smile continues. I am just thrilled with this new discovery.

When we arrive and I deplane, my pain is maybe at a one.

We never did close the sale, but it was one of the most awesome and pleasant business trips I've ever taken.

It is important to me to remind myself of this story over and over.

One of the ways I learn is through experience. For example, if I put my hand out in front of a large black dog and he bites my hand, I may well assume that all dogs bite or at the very least that large dogs bite or black dogs bite. And then, potentially, I may spend the rest of my life afraid of or at least cautious around large black dogs.

If I throw my back out a few times and it always takes months to fully heal and requires special care when sitting, walking, or sleeping along with regular stretching and rehab, I may well assume that this is what will *always* happen when I throw my back out. If this is the only way I learn from experiences, it may well turn me into an opinionated and curmudgeonly old man. My experiences, habits, thoughts, beliefs, and feelings will just get played out over and over and over like a broken record.

Yep. I KNOW how this will play out. And so it does.

But it turns out I have a choice in all of this.

I had a dream years ago while on vacation in Tulum, Mexico. In the dream, I was taken out of my hotel bedroom at dawn down to the Caribbean Sea by about thirty Mayan priests. With the priests all waiting on shore, I walked out and sat down in the shallow, clear water. All the priests were watching me expectantly. A small reef shark swims up and bites my leg and holds on tightly. There is blood and pain. But I just look down at the shark and calmly remove him and say, "I don't have to do it this way anymore." I then turn and swim straight out to sea with all the Mayan priests wildly cheering me on.

It has since become a sort of mantra, "I don't have to do it this way anymore." And life keeps showing me new ways of doing things! It was like in the past I had created some set of fictitious limitations and beliefs based on experiences, and now I have the option of letting them go.

I love the freedom inherent in it. I can change. I can choose to see and experience and appreciate life differently and in a more loving and harmonious way. There is an enlivening vitality I feel in not clinging too tightly to my old ways and expectations.

In one of the Edgar Cayce's books, there is a story about a woman with a long history of migraine headaches. When presented with Cayce's remarkable success in curing migraines, her response was, "Don't be silly. Everyone knows that migraines can't be cured." Yep. It was that same voice in me that I needed to have to courage to override about my injured back.

Since that time, I keep learning new ways for my body to heal—ways that my curmudgeonly know-it-all would never have allowed or even considered as a possibility. I've had experiences that old voice would have said were impossible, nonsense, or make-believe.

Did I know that I could heal my injured back by humming to it? No! But someone or something in me did, and I am so happy that I wasn't too proud or "sure it wouldn't work" to give it a shot. When I got home from my trip, I looked up the lyrics to "Don't Worry, Be Happy." I cracked up when I saw them—the most telling lines were about how worrying makes troubles double.

I'm so happy I didn't choose to worry and make the pain double!

This experience was enlivening and enlightening, and I went to bed afterward, night after night, feeling lighter and happier. To me it was an act of grace. And when I think of it now, that little Mona Lisa smile comes over my face again, and I feel an immense peace.

Yes, peace. Somehow, in that smile, I think she knows a secret that I am only beginning to discover. There is nothing to fear. The universe is friendly and supportive if one has the eyes to see, the ears to hear, and the heart to trust.

81

A Completely Empty Existence

I am having dreams with a consistent theme of emptiness:

- A voice says, *"John, you are headed for a completely empty existence."*
- Another says, *"John, you need to be so empty that you fit through the eye of a needle."*
- At a dream workshop, my only dream is a voice, *"John, leave everything behind. Even your pen."*

I am in a long dark night. "I don't care" seems to be my new mantra. I read St. John of the Cross's "Dark Night of the Soul," and his experience of aridity and of his meditation and prayer suddenly becoming like so many dry brittle leaves, matches my own. There is this sense that I have done something wrong or gone down the wrong path and nothing I do seems to restore that feeling of being inspired or enthused again.

Where did it all go? How do I get it all back?

82

The Little Snowflake

This is a fictional story I wrote in 2014 wherein I was trying to capture the communication between one's unique soul (represented here by the snowflake) and one's ego/personality (represented by the boy/man):

There once was a boy who wanted to catch a snowflake.

On the morning of the first winter's snow, he rushed outside with one of his mother's small frying pans.

It was snowing lightly and sporadically. He looked up and picked out a single snowflake falling from the sky and deftly caught the snowflake in his mother's pan. He rushed to the front porch and took out his magnifying glass and was astonished to see that the snowflake looked like a perfectly balanced, elaborate tiny crystal flower. He loved that snowflake and wanted to keep it forever.

But how, he thought, *does one keep a snowflake forever?*

The boy decided he would sneak into the house and cover the small pan with some foil and hide the pan deep in the back of his mother's freezer. And there the little snowflake stayed for many years.

Until one day, when the boy was a teenager, he heard the snowflake calling to him. Over and over, the little snowflake asked the boy to set him free. The boy was much older now, and even though he still dearly loved his little snowflake, he decided to set him free. After all, the little snowflake had promised the boy he would write, and they would stay friends forever.

The boy dug through his mother's freezer and found the little pan covered in foil, and he took the pan out and walked outside into the warm springtime sun. The little snowflake asked to be set free on the granite outcropping above the small creek that flowed at the edge of the boy's backyard.

He carefully unwrapped the pan, set the pan on its side facing the warm sun, and said goodbye to the little snowflake. The boy watched the snowflake dissolve into a tiny rivulet of running water. It ran down the face of the granite and dripped off the edge and fell into the creek far below.

A couple of weeks went by before the boy received his first letter from the snowflake.

"Thank you so much for setting me free! I have so much to tell you! After I left your mother's pan, I rushed to join many other melting snowflakes. We joined and became a small creek. I loved being a small creek! I flowed through the gills of many fish and quenched the thirst of deer and raccoons.

Soon I joined many other small creeks, and we became a swift river. We joined with the spring force of a billion melting snowflakes and soon swelled into a river of great power. We uprooted many trees and even destroyed the homes of many people.

Eventually our river of great power slowed and merged with an estuary. Life here was slower yet more diverse. The mingling of salt water and fresh water was a strange new experience for me.

And then, I became the ocean. I was so BIG!

And just when I thought my adventures had come to an end, I felt myself rising ever so slowly toward the sky. I was now a "skydrop," and I was joining with many other "skydrops" and rushing inland toward the mountains.

Far in the distance I could see great fires, smoke, and destruction.

When we and all the other skydrops hit the mountains, we all fell at once from the sky into the billowing fires and belching smoke. We snuffed out the raging flames and fed the scorched earth.

As I write to you now, I am feeding the first sprouting of a tiny apple seed.

I have been a snowflake, a creek, a river, an estuary, and an ocean. I have been a destroyer and a healer. I have quenched the thirst of many.

Now I think it is time for me to be an apple tree.

Love,
Your Little Snowflake

Well, many years went by, and the young boy forgot about his friend the little snowflake. But now he was a man, sixty-years-old, and he recalled his old friend and yearned to hear from him again. He was tired and looking to do something new with his life. The many years of pressures and responsibilities in his life had taken their toll, and he missed his old friend.

The next day, a letter arrived from the little snowflake:

"I am the tree at the highest point in the old apple orchard on the east side of the mountain. Please come and be with me."

The next day, the man drove to the old apple orchard and hiked to the top of the mountain. It was late fall and the trees had dropped their leaves, and all looked much alike. Which one was his old friend?

And there at the top he spotted a magnificent *white* apple tree. Its white branches reached for the heavens and its white roots dove far below. Protruding from the wizened trunk was an outstretched white arm and an open white hand.

The man knew exactly what to do. He firmly clasped the hand with a knowingness and a recognition. It was a sincere handshake full of gratitude and appreciation.

The man looked down and found a tiny pile of white seeds in the palm of his hand.

With his heart full, he thanked the old white apple tree, his "little snowflake."

As the man strode down the mountain, he knew he was going to melt. That it was time for him to dissolve again and that it was time for him to share seeds with others and to flow onwards.

His pace was quickening.

He couldn't wait.

83

Space Between Books

I t is 2015, and I'm having a short dream . . .

I see myself taking all the books off my bookshelves and then putting them back in a strange way. I am placing spacers that are at least a foot apart between each book. When I am done, I don't have nearly as many books on my bookshelves. The bookshelves are mostly space now with very few books.

I think I got what the dream was trying to impart to me. To put more "space" between my books—sort of like eating a meal more slowly rather than wolfing it all down, or maybe eating smaller meals or eating fewer meals. That was my old MO for years. Wolf the food down. Wolf the books down. Devour a lot at high speed. I enjoyed wolfing down life!

A friend once told me, "It took me a year to read *Zen Mind, Beginner's Mind* by Suzuki. I read every day for a year. It's seventy-nine pages. I could only handle a paragraph a day. I sometimes read the same paragraph every day for three days. I think I just scratched the surface."

Wow, I was impressed! But I knew what he meant.

I am learning that some books—especially those of a spiritual nature—can take time to sort of sink in. Maybe slowing down here is a good thing and giving new thoughts and perceptions a chance to anchor and take root makes sense. Maybe I can read a bit less and try to give myself more time to absorb the information and essence contained within.

It's strange how a book or a dream or a spiritual experience can bloom and grow over time if given a chance. I recall one famous spiritual teacher saying that he had a spiritual experience decades earlier that even today he was still trying to unpack. That gave me a sense of peace as I frequently revisit various books, dreams, and spiritual experiences and see them with new eyes. My perception of them and appreciation for them never stops growing.

Now it is five years later. It's the year 2020, and it appears that the space between my books may be growing even more. I had a new dream. It was a woman's voice. She whispered to me, *"Your book education has come to an end, my love."*

Uh oh.

The space between my books is cool, but I still love my books. I love my house filled with books. I love lots of books in lots of bookcases. I have a LOT of books! So many of my best times were encountered with my nose in a book. Even with the growing space between all my books, I still have a LOT of books!

But it has already begun. I am reading a lot less now. It seems like I am reading more out of habit than anything else. Is it time to simply take a break from all the books and all the reading? To just "be" for a while?

Or maybe . . .

Many spiritual teachers have written books and given talks about speaking from "space" or "emptiness" or even from the Universe or the Infinite or from Source rather from mere personal memory and memorized facts.

It seems like a huge leap in trust to speak and learn and grow from this place and to set all the books and information and memorized facts aside. But if that is where I'm going, I'm in. It's a huge blow to my old identity as a man who reads and is well read and who has a ton of cool books, but, hey, it feels energizing and enlivening to try a new way of being and a new identity. Even though I'm already sixty-two years old, I'm not ready to stay stuck and to be rigid and opinionated. I'd like to continue to hang on to a sort of youthful zest and to grow and stay open to new ways of being and perceiving the world.

So, it seems I'm moving from lots of books to lots of space—from hanging on to memories to just trusting in the moment. Like a river, life moves on, always refreshing, renovating, and renewing.

I've always loved rivers.

I'm jumping in—with nary a book to hang on to.

84

Befriending Maria

This story came from a dream I had in 2015:

She is my odd next-door neighbor.

Every morning I would see her dress in black robes and then cover her head with a black veil. Then she would walk out her back door, climb into her small round hot tub, and just sit.

It was hard to gauge her age, but she seemed to be quite elderly.

Day after day after day, her routine was the same: get up, dress in all black, place a black veil on her head, climb into her hot tub, and sit with head bowed—all day long.

I would always turn away.

Last night I had a dream that there were many women—perhaps thousands or millions—all dressed in black, heads bowed, and sitting in hot tubs all alone. They all seemed to be grieving.

I had never spoken to my elderly next-door neighbor before. I was aware the kids in the neighborhood simply called her "Old Mary Ann," but I wasn't sure that was her real name.

The next day I resolved to not turn away and instead to go and meet my odd neighbor. So, after my breakfast, I let myself into her backyard and walked up to her in her hot tub. She could sense my presence. I pulled the black veil back from her face. Her eyes were closed.

We said nothing. I reached out and took her hands. They were wrinkled and frail and her pudgy palms were as soft as the softest pillows.

We said nothing.

As we held hands, she seemed to come alive. Her closed eyes opened ever so slowly and were alight with teary-eyed joy. A broad, slow smile joined her sparkling eyes—as if death and grief and depression were being lifted and a new youthful zest was taking their place.

With sudden swiftness, she climbed out of her hot tub, limped toward her house, and beckoned me to follow her. She made us some tea. Somehow, she seemed to know everything about me—my history, my lineage, my fears, my desires, and my secret thoughts.

She shared that her name was Maria and that she often swam in dark seas of sorrow and grief. I was overcome with a sense of wonder and calm respect for my odd next-door neighbor.

The next morning, I watched Maria dress in black, place her black veil over her head, and climb into her hot tub. But instead of turning away, I felt reverence.

I am welcome in her home now. We sit and sip tea together. We hold hands, and we share. I share my zest and vigor and life. She shares the deepest wisdom born in pain and grief and darkness.

85

Avalanche

Six years had passed since Dr. William Brugh Joy passed away in December 2009, and I missed him. I'd read his two books, *Joy's Way* and *Avalanche*, many times.

My paperback copy of *Avalanche* had poor binding and was falling apart. It was hard to keep all the pages together. So I found a used hardcover copy of *Avalanche* on Amazon and decided to treat myself.

When the book arrived, I was happy to see the book was solid and in great shape, and, unlike the paperback, did not have weak binding and thus would not be falling apart.

Imagine my surprise when I opened the book and saw that Brugh had signed it! It read: *"Crisis Awakens! Brugh Joy 1991."*

Love you, Brugh.

86

Dream Remedy

My body runs hot—I'm one of those guys who wears shorts and T-shirts in winter, who loves to swim in cold water, who thinks seventy degrees is a hot day, and who prefers to sit in the shade. In Ayurveda, the ancient Indian healing system, I am what they call *Pitta*—I have a lot of natural inner body heat. Throw in the off-and-on Kundalini energetics, and I have frequently been sort of on broil on the inside.

It is summer 2015, and it has been unusually warm. I have no air-conditioning in my home (as is true for most homes here in the Seattle area), and I am suffering. My body literally feels like it is inflamed on the inside, and the hot weather on the outside of my body is making me miserable.

I slog through my days cranky and tired and desperate for relief from the heat. I go for swims in a local lake and take cold showers, all of which give me only temporary relief.

Then one night I slip into a dream while cranky and haggard, trying to fall asleep in the muggy heat…

I see someone using a sort of yellowish-orange spice in their food, and I know it is turmeric.

I knew that turmeric was a spice often used in Indian dishes but nothing else. After the dream, I did some research and was surprised and delighted to read that it is a natural anti-inflammatory. So I purchased a bottle of turmeric and started sprinkling it on my meals and stirring it into my water. It took a few days, but my body began to feel more comfortable temperature-wise and definitely less inflamed on the inside.

Perhaps it's a tiny thing to be suffering and have a dream offer you a natural and safe remedy, and yet it's a big thing too. I know that excess or continuous inflammation in the body plays a role in various diseases. What if we could all learn to talk to and listen to our bodies in such a way that the body instructs us on how to care for it? What if we all learned to love and care for our bodies at a young age? What if the body itself could self-diagnose and suggest remedies to keep the body in balance, harmony, and perfect health?

It seems like barring physical accidents, such as broken arms or concussions, that health care would look completely different and be entirely focused on clear communication with the body—and the astronomical costs associated with the current system would plummet.

87

Bewitching Hour

This story came from a dream I had in 2015:

It is early September, and I am fishing on the lower Yakima River below the canyon. It is hot and sunny, and the river here moves very slowly. There are other fishermen here too.

The sun is low on the horizon. The insects will soon be hatching, and as soon as the sun sets, the river's large rainbow trout will begin their "evening rise."

Though it is still hot and dry outside, I can feel the end of summer and the approach of fall. The fields and hillsides are dry and drab. The only life seems to be this beautiful blue ribbon of life-giving water, slicing through the barren hillsides and dry farmers' fields.

This is my favorite time of day: that magical moment when the sun is setting on a clear and warm late-summer evening. An old friend of mine called it the "bewitching hour," and he is exactly right.

While waiting for the sun to set, I was suddenly taken over by a variety of fears and angers that were threatening to crash the peace I was feeling.

Stupid people on Facebook. Fake news. *Grrr...*

There were so many fights to be won. Causes. Things to fight for, and fight against. So many wrongs in the world. The problems were so big, so epic, that fixing them all was like bailing out the ocean with a teacup. Man, I was tired of the battles.

In the midst of my fearful and hopeless anger, I felt a light hand on my shoulder. I looked and there standing next to me was Jesus. I'm in my waders in the middle of the Yakima River, and Jesus is standing behind me with his hand on my shoulder.

He says nothing but reaches out for my hand. I willingly place my hand in his and away we go. We follow the Yakima River upstream. We pass farmers and ranchers. Somehow, we see them, but they don't see us. Farther and farther, we go. The river gets smaller and faster as we approach the mountains.

I feel a bit like Scrooge in *A Christmas Carol* except my Ghost of Christmas Past is Jesus. Though I have no idea what's up, I feel immense gratitude while traveling with him.

On and on we go. We finally stop in a small valley where the river is especially fast and violent. Jesus says nothing, but silently, he is asking me to just observe.

There has been destruction and violence here. I see billboards defaced and buildings with graffiti on them. Criminals are on the run, and the police are chasing them. Occasionally, they meet and clash, and battles ensue. No one sees us, but Jesus and I watch it all.

Then Jesus points to the scene in front of me and he says, "This is not your True North."

I nod.

And with that we head back downstream through the mountains, past the farmers and ranchers, back to where the river broadens and slows. It is at this point that I notice we are both walking on water. I wave to the farmers and ranchers, but no one sees Jesus and me walking downstream on top of the river.

We arrive back at my fishing spot just as the sun drops below the dry hills in the distance.

Jesus disappears.

Not all rivers are the same, but I imagine most start out high in the mountains as mere trickles but quickly become violent, rushing torrents. Further downstream, they slow down a bit and may become "useful" to farmers and ranchers. And, as they near the end of their journeys, they broaden and slow considerably. What I imagine all rivers have in common is that one day they all eventually merge with and disappear into the ocean.

Man and rivers. Perhaps we share a lot in common.

The evening rise has begun now, and I see the noses of trout poking up through the surface of the river, snatching the drifting mayflies and skittering caddisflies off the surface. The sunlight is fast disappearing, and an immense peace has settled over the valley.

Inside my belly I feel warm and happy. I walked on water with Jesus, and he gave me a sort of life review and course correction. My face breaks into a serene smile.

Fighting is no longer my True North.

My new True North was not yet clear, but perhaps the lifespan of a river had something to teach me.

88

Mine, Refine, Polish

It is 2016, and I like to explore. One way I experience this side of me is feeling like I have a sort of creative miner inside me. He spends time deep in the darkest mines, hacking away at tons of solid rock all the while looking for that occasional and special diamond.

A voice came to me in a dream last night. It said:

"Mine. Refine. Polish."

Maybe this is the path of creatives, mystics, writers, artists, and explorers. Sometimes we get cranky when a lot of time goes by picking away at endless rock without discovering any new diamonds! Of course, finding the diamond is only the start. Then one begins the process of refining and polishing the precious gem into something that can be shared with others.

89

Three Choices

I had been experiencing a prolonged period of anger in the last week or so, and Brugh showed up in a dream to guide me:

I see Brugh walking into an outhouse with a loaded gun. He says to me, "Now I have three choices: one, I can shoot my way out; two, I can kill myself; or three, I can GO DEEP."

Again . . . the reminder that the people or things I am angry at are not "out there" so no sense in shooting anyone or anything. But, by going deep within, I can discover and release the real source of my anger. It seems I am a slow student, as I keep forgetting this. I really appreciate and need the occasional reminders!

90

Triump!

November 2016. Election Night. I go to bed fairly early that night. Hilary Clinton was expected to win, but Trump was much closer than most experts had anticipated. I went to bed before anyone called the election—at that point, it was too close to call.

I was awakened at 4:00 a.m. by a dream.

A newspaper boy is walking through downtown with an armful of newspapers. I could see the headline. In big, bold print it said, "TRIUMP!"

I felt certain that Trump had won. I jumped out of bed and went online, and everyone was calling the election for Donald Trump. Pretty cool. I can get my instant national news delivered to me in a dream!

91

Absorbing Integrity

Barbara is a Vedic astrologer. It is an early evening in 2017, and I am on her website, where there is a dizzying amount of information. Way too much for me.

But, as I wade through it, I am struck by how utterly honest she is. She repeatedly shares her personal limitations, the limitations of astrology (called *Jyotisha* in India), and how tricky an astrology reading can be. Language is messy, and every single client has their own level of understanding and development.

Such beautiful TRUTH!

It's almost as if she is doing everything in her power to talk potential clients *out* of getting an astrology reading! What kind of a businessperson is that? But I love it! I love everything she says. Her goal is to have the reading confirm the client's own intuition. And she is clearly helping the client access their own intuition—she really is teaching others how to fish rather than just handing them a fish.

This makes my heart sing. There is so much integrity in her words and actions that I feel like bowing before her feet. My heart swells with love and appreciation.

The next morning, I get up and I meditate. And then suddenly, in my mind's eye, Barbara is standing next to me! I don't know how I know that it is her since we have never met, but I just do. She looks middle-aged, has short brown hair, and is wearing what look like reading glasses. We are both facing east toward the first glimmers of sunrise on the horizon.

And then we fuse. The spirit of Barbara and I join in union. It feels wondrously blissful. What a gift!

I have a hunch that this sort of visual mystical encounter—where the very essence and desired qualities of another person appear and are received by another—is more common than we think. We might not see it, and it might not be weird or woo-woo at all. I think it demonstrates the power of love, gratitude, and appreciation and that these qualities attract all sorts of other qualities that as we grow and mature, we can make use of.

My beloved spiritual teacher Brugh once said that spending time in the heart center and in unconditional love would make one more resourceful and that more resources would become available. It's true. It's almost a cliché now to talk about what one "attracts," and yet—I saw it happen!

And now this essence of honesty and integrity lives within me. It isn't perfect, and it's just a seedling, but it has taken root and the yearning to nurture it, and have it grow, is ever present.

Thank you, Barbara. And thank you to the spirit of love, gratitude, and appreciation—truly profound gifts I am only beginning to understand. They are like doors that once opened continue to say, "Welcome Home."

92

A Cross of Golden Rings

I am meditating. An image presents itself to me:

I see a single golden ring—perfectly round, solid, and substantial—set against infinite darkness. Suddenly, I see a second ring attach itself to the bottom of the first ring. In an instant, a third ring is attached to the top of the first ring. Then a fourth ring attaches itself to the right side of the first ring, and again, in an instant, a fifth ring attaches itself to the left side of the first ring. Below and above. Right and left. This cross of golden rings is all in perfect balance.

And then, in a sort of high-speed staccato, I see more and more rings attach themselves. Their counterparts attach themselves exactly opposite. Top, bottom, left, right. Some even attach in, say, the top right, and their counterparts in the bottom left.

In the blink of an eye, I see this perfectly balanced giant cross made of interlocking golden rings. It is an image of astounding BEAUTY.

What is this image trying to impart to me? What is its wisdom?

My best guess is I am looking at humanity in the act of creation. Each person is whole (the ring), yet they each have a certain expression (where the ring is placed on the cross). That expression is perfectly balanced by another whole person in their own unique expression.

All the rings, like all of life and all of humanity, are connected.

The cross itself contains all the perfectly balanced individual acts of creation, and the sum total is wholeness itself.

A thought occurs to me: *If each act of creation is perfectly balanced by its exact opposite, then why do anything? How in the world would anything ever change?*

We see this in politics. A lot. Where every action is stymied by its exact opposite. For example, when Donald Trump was elected president, I had a profound dream of tens of thousands of women marching and celebrating "the return of the witch." Was the return of the witch, the Angry Woman, and the resultant Me Too movement the counterbalancing rings to rings of patriarchal nationalism?

Again, why do anything? Why try? If everything I do is opposed with its opposite, then why *do* anything? It all seems so hopeless.

I'm not sure I have a good answer. But I suppose it would begin with fully embracing one's own unique expression. Perhaps my job is simply to be myself and let God or life decide how my role, however big or small it may be, is important in the act of creation.

I could go further and explore my intrinsic wholeness. Perhaps I am not just a "patriarchal nationalist" or an "angry woman." Perhaps I am both and/or so much more. I could explore my opposites and embrace my intrinsic wholeness.

Maybe I could see myself not so much in my expression—the action I take in the world—and instead, see myself as that whole and perfect golden ring. I am human, I take action in the world, and I take part in the act of creation. But I am also whole, divine, and indestructible.

Going further, I may even find the infinite peace at the center of the ring, that infinite space, that infinite peace that feels like the eye in the center of a hurricane and that is the death of death.

I am human. I take action in the world and participate fully in the act of creation. I know that every act I take affects the whole and that the ultimate mystery of life may simply be balance. Winter–summer, day–night, high tide–low tide, electric–magnetic.

I am divine, aware of and guiding this human being, and experiencing being human here on earth. I am infinite peace, the center of the ring, the center of all centers, beyond all rings yet holding them all—the peace that passeth all understanding.

93

Thank you, Ramana

I am reading a passage from *A Search in Secret India* by Paul Brunton. I am feeing immense love and peace. In the passage, Paul Brunton (the author) has just met the great Indian saint/ sage Ramana Maharshi, and over time, the author develops a tremendous love and respect for him. The author could feel this "intangible and untellable peace" while in his presence.

Later he has a vivid dream that ends with Ramana telling the author, "When this peace will flow into you, then you shall have to forget your own self, for you will have turned your life over to THAT!"

Paul Brunton would later say that he was transformed by his time with Ramana "from a journalist to a gentle sage." He went on to write more than twenty books.

Later that day, I am musing about how much I loved this dream and this passage and the relationship between Paul and Ramana. I want very much to feel that peace and to witness their relationship and the author's transformation.

I go into meditation and ask for Ramana to transmit the peace to me.

A few minutes go by and then a vision takes hold of me. It looks as if a skywriter used the clouds to write me a message across an infinite expanse of clear blue sky. The clouds say, "I see my consciousness established in the enjoyment and fulfillment of life."

Thank you, Ramana.

94

A Conversation with the Boss

I'd been musing about trying to go to Bruce Springsteen's new play on Broadway. I used to be a *huge* Springsteen fan, and I'd read some reviews of the show, and it sounded really cool and intimate. Bruce is a great storyteller, and this show is different—it is longer on stories and shorter on songs.

I had no desire to fly to New York City—especially in the winter. But just for fun I decided to see if I could find tickets. My hopes were quickly dashed as it looked as if every single show was sold out and the tickets that were available from scalpers ranged from around $1,500 to over $3,000 each!

Ugh.

I'd forgotten that this was a man who once sold out ten shows in ten nights at Madison Square Garden and that the theater he was playing in now was considerably smaller.

Sigh. No Bruce for me.

But last night, Bruce came to me in a dream . . .

I am sitting to the side of the stage and Bruce is telling stories. It looks just like I imagined his show would be in the smaller and more intimate setting. A young man I know named Spencer is seated in front of me. He is oblivious to Bruce and is sort of humming and singing his own songs and his own music.

Bruce stops the show and, with such love and respect, offers Spencer some space backstage to hum and sing his own songs so that Bruce could continue with his show.

Spencer happily goes backstage, and Bruce then breaks into a song of his own called "Growin' Up."

Bruce mouths the words to the entire song very slowly, and the crowd joins in on the chorus of "Ooh… growin' up."

Bruce wrote the song "Growin' Up" when he was a very young man. Now he is an elder. And the gift of the dream was that I could see and feel the song through the eyes of a young man *and* through the eyes of the elder. The young man's version feels like "I am the star in my own movie." The elder's version is "We are both the stars in our own movies. I honor your movie and the roles you play and hold it all with peace, love, and compassion."

Love you, Bruce.

95

A Time to Sell

My company is finally doing well nine years after the long, difficult recovery from the 2008 recession, but it has taken a couple of difficult hits. We recently lost distribution in two big retail chains.

I'm not happy with my business. I'm bored and tired of all the never-ending unexpected problems and details. My right-hand "man," Julie, is tired too and sick of all the logistical issues and problems. She wants to quit.

I spend some time at home and come to the realization that while the money is good now, I want to sell my company. My heart isn't in it anymore. I talk to Julie about staying and helping me prepare the company for sale, and I offer her a stake in the sale. She agrees to stay.

I think like a buyer and begin to reshape my company into one I think a buyer would like to purchase. I own and operate a large consumer products company making branded cleaning and pet products sold in thousands of retail stores nationwide. The first thing I noticed was that I had too many products that simply were not selling very well, so I sold all the slow-selling lines to a closeout company for pennies on the dollar. I wanted my company to be lean and mean and super profitable and one that would be easy to take over. I wanted to sell to a competitor whose company was larger than mine and just have our business be absorbed into theirs.

I took all the lessons I had learned in my life—both in the business school of hard knocks and in all of the sort of inner and outer metaphysical lessons I had learned in the last fifteen years. Then I formed a company sale plan.

I set a price I wanted. It was on the high side but definitely doable.

I made it clear what kind of buyer I wanted. I wanted a "strategic buyer"—meaning I wanted another consumer products company who was already doing what we were doing but was larger than us. A strategic buyer could absorb our business into theirs and be far more profitable than we could alone as there would be tremendous synergies and cost savings in freight, travel, overhead, rent, etc. Focusing on a strategic buyer was risky since it would eliminate as much as 90 percent of all the other potential buyers out there. But I knew we could get a better price for the company that way, and I knew the sale would be easier. It's far easier to sell to someone who already knows the ins and outs of your particular kind of business!

I made it clear that I wanted a no BS kind of buyer. I wanted someone honest and who was a straight shooter. I wanted a simple, clean, and easy sale. I wanted trust.

I wanted to sell to someone who wanted my business—that it was the perfect size and fit for them. I really was looking for that win-win type of transaction.

And I asked that my company sales be on the rise as we prepared the company for sale as most buyers are reluctant to pay full price for a company whose sales are declining.

I promised to do my best to work hard but not worry about the sales process and just trust that I would get the right price, the right buyer, and a smooth sales process.

Julie and I spent the next two years making the company as lean and mean and profitable and as easy to run as possible. And somehow despite the hits we took in 2017, sales began to perk up in 2018 and

2019. Existing product lines began selling better, and we gained new distribution in thousands of new stores with other products.

I interviewed business brokers and investment bankers and attorneys and formed what seemed to me to be an awesome team. They, in turn, began marketing the company, and we quickly found a serious buyer.

The potential buyer's team flew out to meet with us, and I about fell over in my chair when the CEO started cracking jokes with me and others and was very honest, humble, and down to earth. The company wanted to move fast with our acquisition. They had just completed two other prior acquisitions, so they were experienced with the process. They also had almost the exact amount of cash on their balance sheet that I wanted for the company.

The entire sale process took about six months, and although there were a few nail-biting moments, I kept surrendering and trusting that not only was it time for me to move on but also that the universe had already found the perfect buyer for me. I admit, that on more than one occasion, I kept expecting the other shoe to drop, that the buyer would go all "Donald Trump" on me, but it never happened. They were honest, humble straight shooters who never played any games for one moment.

On October 1, 2019, the company sale was completed. And I have never looked back.

I recall various college and NFL football head coaches saying they often took the offseason to see if they still had that "fire in the belly" to continue coaching. I admired the ones who acknowledged that if the fire wasn't there anymore, they walked away, despite giving up fame and lots of money.

I had this gut sense that if I didn't sell my company when I did, that things were somehow going to get worse because my heart and my head were not in the game. I'm so grateful for that tiny voice in me that said it was time to move on, and I'm so glad that I chose to listen to it.

Just three months later, the global pandemic hit and caused massive disruptions in the supply chain and logistical headaches far beyond anything anyone in our industry had ever had to deal with. There were times afterward where I literally kissed the ground and was so happy I listened to the nagging inner voice that said it was time to sell.

96

Starseed

It is November 2017, and I am having a dream . . .

Eugenia Oganova is telling me that it is very important that I get a reading from her but to wait until April of next year.

Man, I've had a lot of strange dreams, but this one was really unusual. I need a reading? From Eugenia—someone I don't really know? And wait six months before getting it?

Eugenia is a spiritual teacher. She is fairly young and moved here from Russia in the 1990s and is living on the East Coast now. I had met her once many years earlier in Seattle, and I had one of her books, but a lot of what she wrote about and talked about seemed way over my head.

Still, the dream was compelling, so I scheduled a reading with her for April 24, 2018.

When the reading began, I told her about my dream and that it was only because of the dream that I had booked the reading. I didn't have anything specific to ask her but did say I was curious about past lives.

Eugenia launched into my reading with distinct Russian firmness and directness. Here is a truncated transcription of what she said:

Past lives are too small for you. Let's look way beyond.

The main soul on this planet is one soul split into many different bodies, and these are the Earthling soul group from the sun. They have no past life experiences anywhere besides here on Earth. These comprise 90 percent of the people here on Earth, and we call them new or young because they have only had embodied lifetimes here on Earth.

There is another group here on Earth called *Starseeds* (sometimes called Light Workers). All souls who are not Earthlings, we call Starseeds. They are not one group of people all from the same place. There are from all over. About 10 percent of the beings here on Earth are Starseeds. Of the Starseeds, about 70 percent of them are Pleiadians, and the rest are from other places. You and I [John and Eugenia] are from other places.

In a way the Solar Council (who oversees the Earth simulation) issues visas to other souls from other places to incarnate on Earth. You have to present what you are bringing to Earth, and the Solar Council decides if what you are bringing will mess up the Earth simulation or improve it. Once you incarnate, you can have your own personal human experience and then later contribute and bring what you are bringing in a more positive sense. We are all a part of this.

This is a part of the Starseed Initiative. Originally the Pleiadians tried to do this—they were the fallen angels who tried to help and rescue humans and then fell in and got karmically trapped and linked to humans and could not get out. In the old ways and in the old mystery schools it was all about the light fighting the dark.

On the planet *today*, Pleiadians are stuck here and many of them are still reincarnating in human bodies. There has been a lot of victimization, persecution, and damage. Now, we, who are a part of the Starseed Initiative, are allowed by the Solar Council into Earth to try something else. Their job is to create a new higher morphogenic field by creating sanctuary spheres.

248

John, this is related to your desire to have your house and yard be a gathering place and sanctuary. You also have monk energy looking for sanctuary that is a part of your mission. This is an energy bubble there that is syntropic. Currently, the planet is entropic. The Starseed Initiative is like being undercover agents who incarnate in human bodies and who vibrate in a syntropic way that is self-sourcing. Maintaining one's vertical tube and unplugging from lower morphogenic fields is what creates sanctuary spheres or bubbles. The more we do this, the more it cumulatively shifts the planet.

Holding the higher 3D is essentially like holding a sanctuary sphere. The hope is that it shifts the lower 3D out of existence altogether into higher 3D. But humans have to choose with free will to be self-sourcing and to not give their power away to another person who will 'rescue' them. If this happens the planet will return to a harmonious syntropic simulation.

We each have a personal mission that we presented to the Solar Council. The Solar Council wants to know if this soul who is applying is compatible with Earthlings and others and will somehow contribute. You can have your own experience in a human body and learn what you want to learn, but you also have to contribute something (this is similar to applying to major universities or libraries where you can come to learn for free but also have to promise to teach later on). One of the ways you may contribute is agreeing to vibrate in a syntropic way here on Earth for a particular period of time. This is a part of the spiritual lineage you are from.

Your soul originated in a species that is called Insectoid. They are part of Angeli (angels) and the Butterfly People (like a big bug but not spider or mantis). Consciousness can be in any form. The Butterfly People and Insectoids are incredible with details as surgeons, engineers and are multi-dimensionally very high up. So you were first Angeli then Seraphim then Insectoid and then Butterfly. This was your first embodied form and first semi-separate consciousness. You were mostly electric (masculine) and precision oriented. Then you graduated and decided to try a humanoid body first as a Pleiadian body (not a human body) on Alcyon.

Alcyon is a big stargate and library and mostly run by Pleiadians (on earth these are your New Age love and light people who are innocent and have grace). But they are not detail or choice oriented and yet their innocence gives them great power. On Alcyon the Pleiadians are more electric and magnetically balanced. You can be an engineer who meditates for example. They're librarians and record keepers. That was where you had your first human-like looking body (on Alcyon). But very different from humans. You were a woman and lived a very long time there and really enjoyed it. You did not accumulate much karma, so you didn't have to reincarnate there but you did because you enjoyed it. None of this made you a Pleiadian—it just means that you played with that energy, and it made you sort of Alcyonian.

That was your first experience with being human-like and mammalian. It was your first experience of nurturing and feeling. You had very little of this in the insectoid form, so it was REALLY interesting to you. Depth of feeling is what you craved, but on Alcyon the feelings are more neutral. Feelings were deep but very neutral—like a monk—with no extreme ranges. On Alcyon the range was –10 to +10. (On Earth it is like -100 to +100). Part of why you came to Earth was because you were so fascinated with feelings and wanted more feeling experiences. Earth's duality is very far apart and thus the ranges are very extreme. In other places, it is more normal for everyone to essentially be vibrating more alike. Everyone is pretty much on the same step. On Earth we have souls who are like preschoolers, kindergarteners, high schoolers, and PhDs all together.

So, you agreed to come to Earth and try to hold that higher vibration that was part of the Starseed Initiative. When you incarnated it felt like HELL. You suddenly realized you had no idea what feelings and emotions really were because of the range. You felt pain and anger. That was what got you stuck here. You originally planned to stay for just one lifetime, maybe a few, but once you got karma you could not leave. That is why you are still here.

Let's stay with the BIGGER PICTURE. In your essence you came as an entity that already knew oneness and the structural state of reality to find the feeling state, the Goddess, the fluid state (again your structural state is already highly developed). That is what a part of your personal journey is. But for you, the feelings need to be connected to meaning and your structure in order for them to make sense. Dreams are the pathway into allowing the fluid experience for you. It's like you get the lines but now you are learning about the space between the lines. That is your drive and what took you through Alcyon. So you have to sort of remember what you know while you experience feelings and being fluid so that they get connected to your higher self.

It was an unexpected and eye-opening reading to say the least. Here are some of my takeaways:

- When I was very young, I was obsessed with insects and, particularly, butterflies. Was this because of some soul memory of being Insectoid and Butterfly People?
- Staying centered and "vibrating higher" is indeed a form of selfless service!
- A huge part of my journey here on Earth is indeed exploring and learning about all things feminine and the Goddess—the body, feelings, intuition, relatedness, etc.
- Masculine structure is my comfort zone and is indeed highly developed. Feelings? Not so much.
- One of the *many* reasons it can be difficult to communicate with others is that some souls are indeed much younger and/ or much older than others.
- My home and land are indeed special, and somehow, I have always known I was meant to be right here.

97

Precognition

I am recalling a dream I had in the summer between seventh and eighth grade:

I am sailing my little Sabot sailboat on Los Alamitos Bay in Long Beach, California. It is late morning; the fog has lifted, and a light breeze is picking up. Coming down the bay, I see one of my best friends, Larry, riding on a light-blue surfboard with an inboard motor. He is straddling the board, and he steers it with his hands—the board pivots around whatever hand he places in the water. We spend the next hour or so racing each other.

When I wake up, I think about the dream a bit. I'm young and not at an age where I pay any extra attention to dreams. But a surfboard with an inboard motor is kind of a crazy thing, and I have never heard of one nor seen one before.

I quickly eat breakfast and hop on my Stingray bike and ride down to the Bay. I drag my sailboat down to the water's edge, rig it up, and set sail. It is early, maybe 7:00 a.m., and there is a light fog.

Mine is the only boat on the water, and there is very little wind—the water is like glass.

Later the fog starts to burn off, the sun comes out, and the breeze picks up.

Coming down the bay in my direction is my friend Matt, on a light-blue surfboard with an inboard motor. He is straddling the board and steering it with his hands. We race each other.

Every single detail in my dream has come true with the exception of the friend riding the board. It is Matt, not Larry—although Matt and Larry are good friends and look like brothers. Yet all other details are shockingly accurate right down to the time of day, the weather, the angle of the sunlight, the light rippling waves on the water, the color of the surfboard, etc.

How can this be?

I ask my mother about it later and don't get much of an answer. It isn't the kind of thing we discuss in our family. So, after maybe a day or two, I don't give it any more thought.

But here I am now more than forty years later, and precognitive dreams are starting to happen with some minor regularity.

For example:

About a year ago, I had a dream about an employee's daughter. In the dream, I met my employee's daughter and her daughter's fiancé in Texas and somehow, I knew that they were engaged to be married. The guy was a big dude from Texas—a full head taller than my employee's daughter. The dream took all of maybe one or two seconds.

I cautiously related the dream to my employee, and she said that her daughter had no boyfriend and certainly wasn't in any position to be married. Oh well.

But a month later she shows me a photo on Facebook of her daughter with a new boyfriend from Texas, and it is the exact same guy I saw in my dream! A few years later they got married.

There are other dreams that have been precognitive that have come true as well. To be sure there are other dreams that have not come true. Sometimes in dreams I see scoreboards with final scores on them like WASHINGTON 52—OREGON 48. These have *never* come true. Good thing I don't bet on football.

Other than opening my mind to the possibility that the future can indeed be known, I'm not sure of the purpose of these precognitive dreams. Most of my precognitive dreams have not been of the we-are-giving-you-a-warning-in-advance variety.

When I saw the movie *Arrival,* it sparked something deep within me. As the credits rolled, I felt elated, knowing that something inside was moved by the movie's central idea: that language can be nonlinear and, from that place, *knowing* the future is normal and maybe even commonplace.

I can't explain how someone can know the future. Except, maybe, just maybe, if it is true that there is just one God, one life, one force behind the myriad diverse life forms, it makes sense that if you put yourself in alignment with "it" that "it" may, on occasion, let you in on what's to come. From the point of view of "me," perhaps God is showing me the future. But if the separate sense of me is dissolved and "I and the Father are One," then I can know the future because I am at one with the one behind everything. If behind everything, there is just one master creator and one's consciousness begins to merge with that, then knowing the future is easy!

98

Soul Cat

I am practicing a new spiritual exercise: I say my full name out loud, slowly with purpose. I say my name as if who I am is the soul—eternal and undying. I imagine myself as light.

"John David Latta."

I really feel into it. I say it as the light inside and surrounding my physical body. I am light. I am the soul. I am grounded in this beautiful human body. I say it with great self-love and reverence. I say it again and again, and each time it feels like sparkly joy.

"John David Latta"

"John David Latta."

"John David Latta."

Glittery, effervescent joy.

In my mind's eye, a wise white cat suddenly appears and looks at me with such love. His white fur is full of sparkly glitter. He informs me that all that glittery self-love and joy repels fleas and other pests.

Perhaps this is the real meaning of being "centered" in one's true identity as light or divinity and that it is a wondrous place of a true and radiant power. The "pests"? They can't touch all that glittery self-love and joy residing in one's true Self.

99

A New Me

I took a class with others last week where we focused on the primary and secondary/influencing archetypes in our lives. My primary archetype was the Explorer and the secondary supporting and influencing archetype was the Sage.

When I signed up, I had a lot of reluctance to choose one or two archetypes to self-define. I could see myself in all the archetypes and didn't want to choose just one or two. In fact, I did not want to self-define at all. I was convinced that I and all others were far more complex than could be described using archetypes.

Yet last night in a dream, whether or not I wanted it, I was given my new self-definition. It was called "The Fisherman and the Lady." It looked like an elegant clay statue of an elephant—like a fat and happy Ganesh—wearing an old broad-brimmed fisherman's hat and carrying a fishing rod. Fused to his left side was a goddess with long blond hair. They were both emerging from something that looked like a newly hatched egg.

As I see it, the fat and happy Ganesh with fishing hat and fishing rod symbolizes both the Explorer (seeker/fisherman) and the Sage (wiseman/old soul). The Sage loves to share wisdom and all good fishermen love to come back and share their stories of the big fish they caught and the ones that got away.

The goddess, I suspect, tempers the Explorer/Sage and brings in feelings, care, love, and relatedness. Even with all his wisdom, the Explorer/Sage can be sort of self-righteous, and she keeps him in check with immense love and compassion and offers her own deep wisdom as well.

If I were forced to self-define with a symbol, I would be very happy to self-define with this image. Perhaps this is the ultimate goal of the Kundalini, and here was a vision of it. Not exactly the union of Shiva and Shakti, as one might see it in Hindu texts, but perhaps my own unique version of the union and balance of masculine and feminine.

100

Ascension Symptoms

For the last couple of weeks, my body has been *so tired*. I go to do something—say rake leaves in the yard—and I barely last ten minutes before I am exhausted. A few days ago, I went inside to take a nap and had this short dream:

> *I see the planet Earth as if I am looking at it from space. Then Earth squeezes out a body—like it suddenly gave birth to a fully grown woman. The woman's body then suddenly ascends upward into space at hyper speed in a blur and ends up at the feet of a tall ancient divine being—a sort of tall white statue of a Christ-like man.*

I think the dream is trying to show me that my body is experiencing ascension symptoms and that my body is going through all sorts of physiological changes. Hopefully, I am expanding and growing in consciousness, but I forget sometimes that the body is joining me for the ride. It is said that Earth herself is ascending to a higher vibratory rate and that a part of that process is the upgrading of all human bodies.

I'm not sure who goes first—if I change and then the body plays catch-up or if the body changes first to accommodate future changes in me or if it all sort of happens at the same time. But I do know with certainty that it is happening, and thankfully, I have learned to just roll with it. Born an action-oriented workaholic, I've had to learn that there are times when I just have to lie down and let things go. Then maybe a week or two later, I'm back to working, biking, hiking, lifting weights, yard work, etc.

It's sort of like "crush" then "adjust." It's been going on for years now and seems to be the new normal.

After the dream, I went to bed and just tried to calm myself and listen closely to my body. What I felt was my body in fear. I could feel it. Strange because my life was calm, and I did not feel upset about anything. But still my body was buzzing with fear.

I began going to bed at night and placing my hands on my heart center, telling my body to relax and that it is safe. Night after night, I would feel this sort of low-grade buzz or anxiety in my body—like I was drinking lots of coffee before bed. After a few days, my body calms down.

Over time, soothing my body before bed becomes a semi-regular practice.

101

A Reading from James Van Praagh

It is the summer of 2018, and my daughter, Kelsey, is in town visiting. We are kicking back in the family room watching an episode of the old TV show *Medium*. Afterward, we talk about mediums and whether they can really talk to the dead.

We watch a video on her phone of James Van Praagh—a world-famous medium. I tell her about the time I met him at a book signing and how when he was signing books, he did little mini ten-second readings on every single person as he signed their books.

I tell her that when I got to the front of the line, he looked at me and asked, "Do you do any healing work?"

I stammered and said, "Well, sort of."

He responds, "You should—you're a healer. Next!"

End of mini reading.

I look at all the books in the family room, searching for the one he had signed for me, but I can't find it. I'm pretty sure it is in my bedroom. Anyway, I randomly grab a book off the bookshelf and reenact the process of me standing in line and James giving me a reading while signing my book.

I look down and am shocked to see I am holding the very book he signed for me! It is called *Growing Up in Heaven*, and he signed it, "To John. Love and Light. James Van Praagh."

102

Songs of Support

When the Kundalini energetics exploded in my body in 2004, the next few years were off the charts in terms of wild and fun energetics, miraculous healings, and heart-expanding experiences. But, as time went on, I had an ever-pervading sense that I was dying, being emptied, being drained of passions and interests and desires and hobbies and bucket lists. I'd never ever had a problem waking up in the morning and knowing what to do on my days off. Now I did.

Over the course of just under a decade, I went from not really believing in God, to a sense of being graced by God, and then to a sense of being abandoned by God. Then I often felt bored out of my skull but had no idea how to replace that boredom. The Ketu dream did help alleviate the anxiety and fear I felt around all the boredom, as even boredom has a purpose, but the boredom would grind on day after day after day.

Strangely, every time I got just a bit too deep in despair, the perfect song would start playing in my head upon waking in the morning. Most were not songs or artists I had listened to when I was younger, so it wasn't as if my mind was pulling from my memory. It was more like an inner DJ would select from an infinite playlist in the sky and select the perfect song to help pick up my spirits. It would usually just be one or two lines from the songs repeating in my head like a sort of mantra.

As of 2018, here's a partial list of songs that randomly popped into my head:

- "Born Free"
- "O Holy Night"
- "This Land Is Your Land"
- "If You're Happy and You Know It"
- "Back in the High Life Again"
- "Nothing's Gonna Stop Us Now"
- "When I Need You"
- "Ordinary World"
- "America the Beautiful"
- "God Bless America"
- "Johnny B. Goode"
- "Om Namah Shivaya"
- "The Lion Sleeps Tonight"
- "The More We Get Together"
- "I Did It My Way"
- "Fly Me to the Moon"
- "Can't Help Falling in Love"
- "Your Love Keeps Lifting Me Higher and Higher"
- "Thing Called Love"
- "Can't Keep My Eyes Off of You"
- "Second Chance"
- "Greatest Love of All"
- "(I Have Loved You For) A Thousand Years"

This was a part of the journey I began to trust and enjoy. There was a sense of being guided and supported. If I got just a bit too much off track and stuck in fear or anger, it was as if some hidden part of myself would gently step in to guide me back and sing to me the perfect song and get me back onto a more harmonious track.

103

A Kirtan with Bhagavan Das

Last night I attended my first-ever kirtan with Bhagavan Das at a place called OmCulture in Seattle, Washington. It was the first time I'd ever sat for hours and done devotional chanting. I was surprised at just how much I loved it and how lulling and altering it was in the best possible way.

I had a short dream this morning where I was reading a letter written in cursive that said, "Two is war. Find Samadhi (oneness with God)." It felt like I was picking up on the energy behind Bhagavan Das's kirtan last night. I remembered something Bhagavan Das had said that I love: "Kali: She is the death of death." Oneness with God would indeed be the "death of death"!

As if to synchronistically reinforce the message, I picked up a copy of Amma's biography this morning (Amma is the Hugging Saint from India who has traveled the world and hugged tens of millions of people) and opened to a sentence that read (I am paraphrasing) *that everything disappeared into a sea of light.*

104

Spiritual Housecleaning with Michael Singer

People sometimes sit with spiritual teachers because they carry a certain energy that is sometimes felt as peace, bliss, love, or joy. Many come to be with spiritual teachers not so much for new facts and information but just to immerse in the energy of the teacher.

It is November 2018, and I sat with Michael "Mickey" Singer last week at his Temple of the Universe in Alachua, Florida. Over and over, he talked about simply witnessing thoughts and emotions—that each person is the witness, and when difficult emotions, troubling thoughts, and memories come up to simply witness them, allow them to release, and let them go.

Later that night, after meeting "Mickey," I have a dream . . .

Michael Singer and I are in my "house" on top of a mountain and a powerful windstorm comes and blows a bunch of my stuff away—including some fishing books I was working on.

Later, I have a second dream . . .

A voice tells me that some people's "service" to the world is that they are "spiritual house cleaners."

I suspect that spiritual housecleaning might be one of Michael's gifts of service to the world and that maybe being in his presence helped blow away some of my old "stuff." I wasn't swooning in peace in his presence, but I did feel unburdened, lighter, and happier upon returning home to Seattle.

105

What Are the Odds?

It is September 2018, and I had a dream last night:

I catch a tiny baby garter snake in my house, toss it out on the lawn, and then watch as a larger snake attacks the baby snake and quickly eats it.

Tonight, I am home watching a football game. I get up to use the bathroom and just outside the bathroom door in the corner of the family room is a tiny baby garter snake (maybe just four inches long) caught in a small spiderweb on the floor. The itty-bitty snake is furiously trying to escape, but it is so small that it can't escape the web it is trapped in. (I promise I keep a clean house and don't usually have snakes and spiderwebs in it!)

I pick up the snake and go to throw him out on the lawn but mindful of my dream the night before I instead carefully place him in some bushes.

What are the odds? A tiny garter snake? Stuck in a spiderweb? In my house?

And I had a dream about this the night before? How is this even possible?

106

Sprouting Wings on
the Hands of Time

This story, which I wrote in 2019, came from a dream:

I am a student here at a large public university. I have been here for a few years studying theology, philosophy, and history. I've learned a lot, but now I've lost interest.

This morning I go to grab my backpack, and to my dismay, it is gone. I know who took it: an older Indian man—balding with mischievous eyes—has been following me for weeks.

My precious backpack—full of textbooks, homework, research, papers, journals, pens, notebooks, my laptop, years of work—all gone. I know it was that darn Indian man, sneakily following me everywhere. But now, he and my backpack are gone.

I've already looked everywhere. Sigh.

Everything.

Gone.

I sit with slumped shoulders, oozing despair. I decide to go to the campus store but have no enthusiasm. I simply don't want to be here anymore. But I walk toward the store anyway.

I look up and the giant clock at the top of the clock tower looming over the campus says it is 11:00 a.m., but it is dark outside. Even weirder, the hands on the clock are starting to go backward.

I walk into the campus store to buy a new backpack, more books, etc. But the store is dark and crowded, and people are fighting over the best stuff. The selection is poor.

I leave the store. I don't want to go to this school anymore.

I've already lost everything. Why not just leave?

I feel no love, no joy, no creativity, no inspiration here anymore.

There must be a different way. I don't know what it is yet, but it isn't here.

So I leave. The store. School. My precious education.

Then my slumped shoulders straighten up. I suddenly move swiftly and easily across campus. I have a bounce in my step and fairly glide across campus. The other students stare at me with wonder and curiosity as I look like a happy astronaut lightly bounding across the surface of the moon for the first time.

The sun comes up. I look up at the great clock atop the looming clock tower. The hands on the clock sprout wings and move swiftly forward.

I have nothing. I have no idea where I am going, but I'm full of a new sort of joyful open anticipation. I feel it in my belly.

Someday I may bump into that mischievous Indian man again— the one who stole my backpack—and bow down to him in immense gratitude.

107

A Psychic Physical

It is 2019, and my new girlfriend, Wendy, is a health fanatic. She wants me to go see her naturopath and get a full physical. I am sixty years old, and I think I am in good shape for my age. I don't want to get a physical and don't think I need one. I have been living with this intention and belief that my body will tell me when something is off, and I will listen to it. But it wouldn't hurt to get a physical as it had been over a decade since my last one, and in the interest of my new relationship, I agree to go.

When I schedule my appointment, Wendy asks me to tell the doctor that I want a full physical and to have the doctor check on my testosterone level. Wendy says there are pellets that can boost testosterone.

Later I think about it and I'm a bit miffed—does she think I have low testosterone? Am I not manly enough? Do I not have enough physical and/or sexual energy? My inner knowing says I am fine but since I am sixty years old now, maybe I *should* have this checked.

I go and give blood, saliva, and urine about a week in advance of my scheduled physical. A few nights before my physical, I have a dream:

I am seated in a doctor's office. I see what looks like a Middle Eastern woman with medium-length dark brown hair put on a lab coat and then walk up to me. She is looking at my lab charts and then she says to me, "Well, you definitely don't need the pellets."

After the dream, I'm all excited and can't wait to go to my appointment and see if the dream is true.

I arrive at the doctor's office and am assigned a room. My door is open. I see what looks like a Middle Eastern woman with blond hair put on a lab coat and walk up to me with my lab charts. She introduces herself as Dr. Kimiai, and she is studying the charts and says, "Well, you definitely don't need the pellets."

Every single detail in the dream came true except my doctor had blond hair and not dark brown hair. Later, I get home and tell Wendy about my dream and my experience, and she says, "Wait. Dr. Kimiai dyed her hair blond?"

Apparently, between the time I had the dream and my actual appointment, my new Persian doctor had dyed her hair blond!

I love psychic dreams and premonitions, and I never know when they will come or why. There was no urgent message for me in this case. It simply confirmed what my inner knowing was telling me— that I am fine and healthy. I simply got an advance preview of what was to come in my meeting with the doctor. Perhaps more startling to me was not the message but that the future played out almost exactly as it had in my dream. I love it, but I still can't wrap my puny brain around how it happens!

108

Origin: Paradise

It is 2019, and I had this dream last night . . .
I am staring at the cover of a book and the book is entitled BORN IN PARADISE—STUCK IN A SANATORIUM.

109

Something True

It is 2020, and for about the last five or six years, I have hosted an event in our home that I call SOMETHING TRUE. We have a potluck dinner, and afterward, we circle up, create a warm heart-centered space, have a short meditation, and then we all take turns simply checking in and sharing what is going on in our lives with as much truth, honesty, and fearless vulnerability as we can.

I have been a part of a men's organization called ManKind Project (MKP) for many years now and the email invitations to the event go out to our local MKP community email list and my own personal email list plus all of my Facebook friends. In all, the invitations go out to about 1,000 people. I tell everyone that the event is free, and they are welcome to bring friends, spouses, family, or partners.

I have held this gathering about twenty times. Weirdly, we always get a gathering that is just the right size. I can comfortably get up to about thirty people in my family room sitting in an oval circle shoulder to shoulder. One time we had forty people (some had to sit on the floor or on laps), and a few times we got about eighteen. But generally, we always get about twenty to twenty-five people.

They are not all the same people. Maybe a quarter of the people who come are complete strangers (to me anyway). A few come every time. Some maybe once a year. Some bring friends, family, or spouses. One couple brought a young couple with them that they'd met at Burning Man the week before. One guy brought thirteen men at the last minute who were going through a weekend of MKP training. There have been attendees representing all ages, all sexes, many nationalities, and many different religious cultures.

If everyone who was actually invited came, there would be more than 1,000 people. If they brought friends and spouses and family members, there would be well over 2,000. Talk about a sense that there is some sort of greater mystery at play. Some greater force knows exactly how many people will fit in the family room and indeed selects the perfect mix of people. We always seem to get the perfect number and the perfect mix. How is this possible?

Such a joyful mystery.

110

The Great Spiritual Human Teacher

This story, written in 2020, came from a dream:

I'm up front in a crowd of hundreds of people here in Seattle. We are all listening to a great spiritual teacher. She is intelligent, aware, and awake. Her talk is riveting (although maybe a bit over my head). But somehow, I know that she just *knows*, and I'm grateful to be here.

She is a friend of mine, and I'm happy to host her appearance here in town.

A man in the audience asks my famous spiritual teacher friend a question: "Can you tell us about your childhood and your life growing up?"

She pauses and begins to falter a bit and tear up. I smile at her and, good host that I am, I jump up on stage to help. She looks at me expectantly. I tell her it's OK for her to cry. I offer her a box of tissues.

The crowd is supportive and encourages her. "Yes, we want to hear about your childhood and your life story."

My great spiritual teacher friend is reluctant. She is appreciative of the support but says her life and childhood stories "don't scale very well."

It's true. They don't.

How to describe a childhood filled with regularly speaking to beings from other worlds and other dimensions? Of being a child who was awake and aware of her past lives and the past lives of others? Of her regularly speaking with deceased relatives? Of her many and varied precognitive dreams? Of knowing the thoughts and intentions of others? Of seeing human auras so clearly that childhood friends could never truly hide in hide-and-seek because she could always see their energy fields—even behind walls and closed doors? Of being paraded before others like a circus freak by her own parents? How to explain the hours upon hours spent creating code in the form of lattices of light surrounding the planet Earth?

Not exactly a normal life nor a normal childhood.

I sit down next to her and encourage her to try. Spiritual teachers are always pushing boundaries beyond the collective norm, and nearly all spiritual teachers have, at times, endured great suffering.

While her stories might be hard to grok and be difficult to relate to, we can probably all connect with, at times, being misunderstood, being labeled as freaks or weirdos, and perhaps never getting any acknowledgment for our unique intelligence or perceptions.

So, she looks at me, takes a deep breath, and then decides to share her stories with the crowd. In so many ways, it was her best talk ever. Her full range of divine resources, wisdom, and awareness were on full display—yet in a very human body with a very human story and with very human feelings. The crowd cried. The crowd cheered. We all left cracked open in the best possible way.

Up to that day, it never occurred to me to have compassion for people who were spiritual teachers and who were intelligent and awake.

I went home that night full of gratitude. Grateful for the entire experience and grateful for the realization that we ALL—every single one of us—deserve compassion. Being human. Being in density.

Living in a world with a range of duality that is extreme. Living out patterns and karma and roles and archetypes. Billions of people somehow all living together and all with their own unique perceptions and beliefs. Probably, for most of us, our behavior and our choices are mostly *unconscious*!

What a crazy, beautiful, horrible, and amazing journey it can be to live a human life!

111

To Boise

My fiancé, Wendy, and I are near the tiny town of La Verkin in southern Utah. We have been on a long cross-country road trip for about two months—right near the beginning of the COVID-19 pandemic. We have been staying in Airbnbs for about a week at a time and then moving on.

At the moment, we are sitting on the ground of a narrow, wooded trail discussing where we should go next. We have been all the way from Seattle to Florida and are working our way back toward the Seattle area. We had a home booked in Boise, but the owner canceled on us. The virus has made travel and lodging difficult and unpredictable.

When we first began planning our trip, we decided to not over-plan and to allow as much spontaneity and flow into our trip as possible. Little did we know that a full-blown pandemic would enshroud us in constant uncertainty and force us to sort of make the trip up day by day on the fly. What planning we did make prior to leaving was all thrown out the window. But we were discovering that even amidst all the uncertainty and dismantling of all our advance planning a lot of magical things kept happening.

So we are discussing whether we should head home via Jackson Hole, Yellowstone, and Missoula, Montana, rather than going home though Boise. We had wanted to stay in Boise and spend time hiking up near Bogus Basin but, regrettably, didn't see any other available Airbnbs in that area. Going through Yellowstone would be fun, but April weather can be dicey there. We weren't sure what to do.

Five minutes into our discussion, an older couple walks up to us on the trail. They are open, friendly, and talkative. The virus has emptied the hiking trails and the ones who are still out hiking tend to turn away in silence. It is nice to talk to real people in person who want to engage. The couple is also on a long road trip but traveling in their RV. We share some road trip stories in the era of the global pandemic, and then I share that we are trying to decide whether to go home through Yellowstone or see if we could change our travel dates and try to find another place in Boise.

Turns out the couple was from Boise! They insisted we spend time in their town. They told us all the best places to go and urged us try to find a home on the road to Bogus Basin. We figured we would give it another shot. Back at our rental in La Verkin, Wendy and I searched again online and, to our surprise, found a perfect place to stay in Boise on the road to Bogus Basin. We thoroughly enjoyed our time there.

Synchronicity. What are the chances? Boise is over 600 miles from La Verkin, Utah. We were on a mostly vacant trail—we walked by maybe one or two people an hour. We are trying to decide whether or not to go home through Boise. The only people who stopped to talk to us were from Boise and extolled all the benefits of going there and all the fun things to do on the way to Bogus Basin. My love of synchronicity deepens.

112

My Soul's Desire

I was reading a book with my wife, Wendy, last night, and the author was talking about asking what the soul wants (rather than the ego/personality). So, as I prepared for sleep, I asked for a dream to show me what my soul wants, and I had the following dream:

> I am lying under a blanket in a room with maybe one hundred people in it. The moderator asks an elderly Buddhist Asian man wearing crimson robes to talk about anger. He is intelligent and analytical and yet having a difficult time explaining anger to the crowd and gets visibly frustrated that no one understands what he is attempting to teach.
>
> The moderator then asks me to talk about anger. I'm caught off guard, as I was not expecting to be called on. I sit up and explain that I have a lot of fire and warrior energy in my astrological chart and that quick and reactive anger is pretty normal for me. I'm a fiery guy. I say that the only thing that seems to work for me is to quickly catch myself and just notice, "Hey, I'm angry" and that somehow this calm look within and then sort

of observing the anger rather than getting swept up in it works best to unhook me from it.

As I am talking to the crowd, I notice I am going deeper and deeper into feeling and seem to speak best when I keep my eyes closed and speak from this level. I feel calm and centered as I just sit and feel anger rather than explaining it or defining it. I acknowledge the anger but don't intellectualize or rationalize it. I'm not getting angry, but I'm also not pretending that there is no anger. In this peaceful looking within, I note that I am not afraid of the anger.

I feel like I should open my eyes to be polite to the group, but, for some strange reason, I can't see anyone when I open my eyes. So I just keep my eyes closed. It's peaceful speaking this way but also vulnerable—since I can't see their facial expressions, I have no idea what people are thinking of me. But with my eyes closed while remaining open and vulnerable going within, I feel honest and sincere, and when I finally do open my eyes, it is clear that what I had to share was well received by the crowd. This surprises and delights me.

So, my soul wants me to go deep. With feeling. Share with others. In an open and vulnerable way. Fearlessly. In total trust. And to know there is immense peace behind anger. Sounds easy. But it isn't always easy for me to do this nor easy to remember. I forget.

But there is something magical about speaking in this way and from this deeply rooted, honest, and centered place. I feel the connection and the magic when others speak from this place, and when I remember to speak this way, others can feel it too. It is a rare, vulnerable intimacy wrapped up in a beautiful and radical sincerity.

So now I will try to remember. A message from one's soul—a simple piece of guidance—is a precious thing. I'm grateful for all the men and women in my life who already speak in this way and who help remind me what an amazing world it would be if we all could speak and share like that.

113

Feelings, Compassion, and Forgiveness

My wife, Wendy, and I were having an argument. It was not a big thing, but somehow it seemed to be the same argument we'd had before dressed up in different clothes. She would ask what I thought was a literal question. So, I would give a literal answer. The end.

Except to her it wasn't the end. It wasn't over. It wasn't complete. In her mind, she had not asked a "literal" question. To her it was a question laced with feelings and an intuition that, at the moment, our deep bond and connection had been severed. She grew agitated and frustrated and asked more literal questions. I answered them with more literal answers, and my own agitation and frustration grew.

While this pattern was not a daily occurrence, it was happening often enough that I knew it was a problem. Talking it through and sharing our points of view and perspectives was not helping much and only seemed to make matters worse. I went to bed that night determined to try and shift things.

I knew about the power of compassion and forgiveness. I lay in bed, and with as much intention and sincerity as I could muster, I asked for the grace of compassion and forgiveness. I forgave myself for sometimes being so literal minded. I forgave my wife for being frustrated with me at times. Then the forgiveness went deeper.

Somehow, I could feel that I was asking for compassion and forgiveness on the part of me and on the part of all literal-minded men throughout history. We simply sometimes did not grok the language of feelings, and because we could not understand it, we could not see the value in it. Then I could feel myself apologizing to my wife and indeed to women throughout history—there were times I simply did not understand, and they, in turn, were not understood. Whether it was intentional, cultural, a habit, or the wiring of my male brain and many other men's brains, literal and logical were not always in coherent, continual communication with feelings.

And then most amazing thing happened.

In my mind's eye, I saw what looked like a road that stretched from far back in history. Thousands of women were walking the road from way back right into my heart center. There was a sort of overwhelming sense that somehow in the act of asking for compassion and forgiveness, I could feel all of womankind's pain and suffering throughout the centuries in not being understood at the level of feeling, that what was a natural expression for many had been squashed for countless centuries. The experience went on for a full ten minutes. It was like a hyper-vivid dream of all the misunderstood women throughout time somehow returning Home via a very long road right into my heart center.

In asking for compassion and forgiveness, I was graced.

But now the real work has begun. The experience of compassion and forgiveness was awesome and awe inspiring. But a single awe-inspiring experience is often just the beginning and not the end. So I'm trying to be more aware now of the language of feelings. I'm trying to be more aware of what language my wife and others are speaking so that I might be better able to understand and communicate. I'm learning to value the language of feelings. I'm capable of feelings and understanding feelings, but sometimes I override them. Being logical and literal is a well-entrenched habit, but habits can be changed with time, sincerity, and discipline.

So, I'm intent on being more in the state of feelings and learning to speak and listen from this place. I'm intent on being more aware of when others are speaking and listening from this place so that we can better communicate. I'll keep practicing so that it becomes a new habit.

Compassion and forgiveness. Sometimes I just forget, but I'm working on making them new habits as well.

114

Reaching the Top with Wendy

Wendy and I met just two years ago in 2019, and it seemed like we had decade's worth of experiences and sharing with each other all in the first year. Wendy had experienced a traumatic loss in a recent previous relationship and was still anxious and vigilant. I sold the company I had owned for thirty years. Wendy sold her house and moved in with me. We took a nearly three-month long road trip from Seattle to Florida and back and managed to leave right after the pandemic hit. There was this sense that if there ever were such a thing as soul mates, we had found it here with each other. I'd never felt such a sense of ease and trust and love and harmony between myself and another. Not ever.

But every now and then, an argument would come out of nowhere. Most of the time we seemed to communicate with great ease, but occasionally, there would be a massive misunderstanding, and all sorts of entrenched and ancient fears would erupt. There seemed to be a pattern—great love and fun and joy and harmony and then maybe once every six weeks or so an argument would happen, and instead of lovers, we would look like two soldiers dug in and prepared to fight for a very long time.

It was exhausting. In a way we both seemed powerless to stop it. Then I had a dream . . .

I am driving a car with Wendy up an impossibly long, steep hill. The hill is miles long and nearly straight up and down. Looking back and down behind us, I could see it was terrifyingly steep. But we were arriving at the top now, and the road was beginning to flatten out, and it was beautiful up here—sunshine, woods, and lush green grass—like a magical woodland park at the top of a very high hill.

The dream soothed me.

Wendy and I really had come a long way fast and had driven up an impossibly steep hill. Things were going to get better. The road was flattening. We were almost at the top. It was beautiful up here. I knew we were going to be OK.

115

Fall City

Nearly two decades ago, I had the strangest experience. I had a full book "downloaded" into me in a split second. The book was entitled *Fall City*. I knew all the characters, the setting, how the story opened, what would happen, and how it would all end.

I was tremendously inspired and determined to put the story on paper. The downloaded book was set in Fall City—an actual small town about thirty minutes east of where I live. On my next day off from work, I drove out there and took detailed notes about the town.

I was so psyched and excited to write my first book! I raced home, and with as much care as I could muster, cranked out eight pages on the first day. I was so pleased with my first effort! I'd never written a fictional story before.

The story was about a rich doctor from Seattle whose wife had died. He was lonely and decided to sell his practice and buy the old Fall City Inn perched on the banks of the Snoqualmie River where he used to steelhead fish in the winter. He let his intuition guide him and remodeled the old Inn into a BNB. He only had four rooms, but strangers from all over the world would come for a weekend, and the doctor would be their host and do all the cooking. But the old Inn had a certain magic, and the guests who came would have powerful dreams they would share and that would draw everyone together in a sort of magical, loving, and healing synchronicity. I even wrote myself into the story calling myself "John Payne."

After writing my eight pages, I went to bed with a happy smile on my face. But when I woke up in the morning and read what I had written the day before, I HATED IT! I was full of fear and revulsion. It felt like I had gotten drunk the night before and spent the night making love to a beautiful woman only to discover she was someone else entirely the next morning, and I was lying completely naked next to her. I was definitely having what I later learned is called a "vulnerability hangover."

For a first try at writing a book, the writing seemed OK to me. But it felt like I was revealing too much about myself and my inner world in the writing of the story. Over and over, I would read it and be horrified. It felt like those dreams of walking down a crowded city street completely naked with everyone staring. I was terrified. I hid the story so no one could see it.

I never wrote another page of that story. But in my sort of slow-motion way, I began to heal my inner creative artist.

A friend suggested I read *The Artist's Way*, a twelve-step recovery program for recovering one's inner creative artist and muse. I joined an Artist's Way group. It was the first time I had ever shared anything I had written. I tried writing true stories, fiction, and poems; I tried drawing and painting. It helped tremendously, and I have reread *The Artist's Way* cover to cover and worked the program on multiple occasions.

I often get impatient with change—in myself and in others. But something so natural as being creative or artistic was so deeply buried in ancient eons of staying in hiding that bringing it back out again has been long and slow and arduous.

I recall Michael Roads, author of *Talking with Nature*, stumbling into the gift of being able to communicate with all of Nature. But he was an impatient and impulsive Aries and had been a crusty, cranky old farmer and could not see how he could possibly share this "gift" with anyone. He could not see the value in it, nor could he stomach the idea that others would think he was strange. I thought it was incredibly cool. But he battled fear and self-doubt about sharing his gift for many decades.

It has taken me a very long time to get up the courage to share my life and my stories here in this book. But it's all good. It's helped me develop patience and compassion in healing and transformation. It taught me that healing and integration are full of great joy and sometimes great fear, self-doubt, and unexpected difficulties. Certainly, everyone I have ever known who has transformed themselves and grown in all the most positive ways has also encountered self-doubt and fear about one's new identity, and all this struggle to assume a new identity can also be incredibly difficult on relationships.

Tonight, I am rereading the eight pages I wrote back in 2003. *Fall City*. Even in the mere eight pages I wrote, I can see patterns that played out in my life and the identity changes that were begging to happen and indeed did happen. It's a good story. It's a true story.

Here is the unedited story exactly as I wrote it eighteen years ago:

FALL CITY
By John Latta

Chapter 1

John Payne left his home in Redmond, Washington at 5 pm on Friday night headed for the old Fall City Inn. Recently divorced and with custody of his 2 children Sean, age 12 & Kelly age 10, he was headed to Fall City for a break. His separation and consequent divorce from his wife of 12 years had caught him by surprise and he was still struggling to live the life of a 44 year old working single parent. Fall City, at the confluence of the Raging River and the Snoqualmie River would give him a chance to get away, do a little steelhead fishing and just plain relax. He'd driven by the Fall City Inn dozens of times and since the innkeeper made all the meals and the rates were low, he decided to treat himself.

Lori DeBartolo was vacationing in Seattle with her folks. In the middle of an ugly divorce, Lori left her home in New York and was in Seattle to find time by herself to sort things out. Her parents had always been there for her and even though she was 40 years old and this was going to be her second divorce, they were here in Seattle with Lori giving her all the support she needed. But Lori needed to escape for a few days even from her parents so she planned to leave her folks at the Westin Hotel in Seattle while she hid away at the Fall City Inn.

Another attorney in a long line of attorneys in the family, David Jones was in Fall City on business. He'd just completed a lengthy interview with a client in the wealthy new Snoqualmie Ridge development. He had mountains of paperwork to catch up on and planned to stay at the Fall City Inn and work in his room rather than returning to his office in the Columbia Tower in downtown Seattle.

Still struggling to put her life back together, Liz Peal was coming to Seattle to visit her sister, Michele. Liz's life had been marred by tragedy and she left her home in Colorado because Michele was the one person she could count on for solace. She wouldn't be meeting Michele for a couple of days and her sister recommended the old Fall City Inn.

Patrick Callahan, affectionately known as "Paddy" by the locals, was the sole owner and proprietor at the old Fall City Inn. His little Inn had only 4 guest rooms and he did all the cooking and cleaning for his guests. Meals were big and served family style.

Locals joked that Fall City was a "passing thru" town. Everyone passed thru Fall City on the way to get somewhere else. A tiny little strip town perched on the banks of the Snoqualmie River, about the only reason anybody ever stopped here was to do a little steelhead fishing in the river. Most were passing thru on their way to Interstate 90, or on their way to Snoqualmie Falls. Some were headed into the Snoqualmie Valley to pick strawberries or to visit local dairies or take in the pretty valley views. Occasionally, the river would flood the valley and throngs from Seattle would take the short 30 minute drive out to witness Mother Nature's fury. But most of the time, Fall City sat there while time and everybody in their cars passed it by.

At the base of the Cascade Mountains, Fall City gets rain & lots of it. It was January now and the foothills had low sullen looking clouds clinging to the hillsides. It was nearly dark and the sky looked like more rain was coming.

John Payne, Lori DeBartolo, David Jones and Liz Peal would be Paddy's guests at the Fall City Inn this weekend. Paddy served his meals family style and dinners were served promptly at 6 pm. This being Friday night, the 4 guests all arrived at the last minute, a bit harried from their long travel and their workdays.

"Jeez, I can't believe this spread. And this guy does this all by himself?" said John. John was a fitness fanatic, lean and always hungry. "Salmon, pasta, jasmine rice, Caesar salad, fresh warm French bread, gosh, I'm starved. Hi, I'm John Payne."

"I'm Lori and just flew in this morning from New York. My folks are with me but I left them in a hotel in Seattle and I'm sort of hiding out here for the weekend."

"David Jones. Pleased to meet you all."

"Hi John, David & Lori, I'm Liz Peal."

Paddy, red faced and grinning from ear to ear, was a short dumpy little man, mostly bald and was racing back & forth bringing out dish after incredible looking dish from the kitchen. After he set the last dish on the table he said "I know none of you are officially checked in but dinner is served now and I'll get you to your rooms soon enough. Please sit down & let's eat!"

The big heavy wooden table was round and the 4 guests and Paddy all seated themselves around it. John wasn't shy and he grabbed the first dish and started filling his plate.

Conversation was led by John who didn't seem to care that nobody knew each other. They talked a bit of their lives and why they had come to the Inn for the weekend. David & Lori haggled over politics and before long, the 4 guests all looked over at Paddy and John spoke for all of them.

"So Paddy, enough about us. You look like you know something. Tell us about you and this Inn."

All thru dinner Paddy had this silly little grin on his face, like he'd been sneaking sips of wine in the kitchen or perhaps that he had a little secret.

"Fucking idiot" thought David. "Why's he always smiling?"

"Well, I used to be a physician and a very good and respected one in Seattle" said Paddy. "I worked my tail off though and never really got to see my 2 children grow up because I was working so much. When I was 50 years old, my practice began to mean less and less to me. My daughter had moved to Europe and I never saw her. My son Nick was an airline pilot and then out of the blue his plane crashes. My wife Mary and I are so fraught with grief that we never seem to get over it. And then Mary gets breast cancer and dies 6 months later. Life seemed so barren to me after that so I sold my practice and sort of floated thru life without a rudder."

"Well, I used to come down to the river here in Fall City to do a little steelhead fishing in the winter and started coming down here more & more after Mary and Nick had died. After we get all our gear on...stocking hats, waders, fishing vest, Gore-Tex coats and grab our rods and wade into the river we all really look alike. It didn't matter that I was a rich big shot doctor from Seattle. Down here on the river we were all one. The river, the camaraderie helped me feel & think about things."

"One day, about 15 years ago, I'm fishing with the locals and they say the old Fall City Inn is up for sale. Apparently, it was family owned and some family members had died in a fire and now the Inn was up for sale. Suddenly I feel these very strong urges to check this place out. I envisioned me cooking for and visiting with guests and that strongly appealed to me. I liked cooking and had been around people my whole life in my practice and suddenly I missed that."

"So, I moved fast. I bought it for a fair price, sold my big fancy home in Seattle and moved in here. I sort of let my intuition guide me in remodeling the place but just felt electric about what I was doing.

I never advertised and just figured word of mouth would spread that I've got a pretty special place here. It's been 15 years now and though I still grieve for Mary & Nick every day, I've never been happier."

"Fucking idiot" snorted David to himself. "Walking away from his practice to run this place"?

John couldn't quite put it into words be he knew that Paddy knew. "But knows what?" John thought to himself.

Lori just cried & cried when she heard Paddy's story and Liz felt a certain wordless connection to this funny little old man.

The guests helped Paddy clear the table and then Paddy said it was off to bed for everyone. Paddy took over. "All of the 4 rooms are decorated exactly the same so please just grab whichever room suits you. We are an early to bed and early to rise Inn so please go to sleep and plan on a big breakfast at 7 am sharp. The sun, when you see it, which is rare, rises at about 8:30 am and sets about 4:30 pm."

"I've built huge crackling fires in your rooms that should burn most of the night. All of the rooms have oversized stone fireplaces and when they burn, the river rock gets hot and radiates heat all night. You might want to open your windows and let some of the cool night air in. You all have big beds with lots of blankets so you'll have no trouble keeping warm. With your windows open you'll hear the rushing river and the falling rain. The rhythms of the water and the crackling fire will lull you into a very deep and peaceful sleep, something I'm sure you all could use."

"One more thing...listen closely for the Call tonight. If you relax and listen closely, perhaps you'll hear it. Now, off to bed and sweet dreams!"

"Fucking Idiot" whispered David. "Call of what? Are there wolves around here or something?"

"I don't know what he was talking about" murmured John, "but I'm ready to crash. My own fireplace with a big roaring fire in my room sounds great."

Lori was still crying as she lugged her bags to her room and Liz seemed lost in thought as she too gathered her bags.

David Jones had just two bags; one with a change of clothes and the second with all his paperwork. He walked in the room and threw his bags down. David was not easily impressed but the massive stone fireplace in his room had the mother of all fires going in it. "Pretty impressive" thought David. It was warm in the room. Too warm, so David threw open the window. Rain had just begun falling and he heard the river rushing by and the steady drumbeat of the rain. It was pretty cozy in here he thought and the massive bed and the huge pile of blankets looked inviting. He leaped into bed with the paperwork from the client's interview earlier today but quickly set it aside as a wave of sleepiness overtook him. So he took off his glasses and set aside all the paperwork. "No problem," he thought, "I have all weekend to complete this and with the old man cooking for me I'll have plenty of time to finish my work."

David was reaching for the light when he suddenly noticed the massive painting above the fireplace. He was transfixed and just stared at it. It looked like a massive muscular completely naked Native American was perched at the top of Snoqualmie Falls and was sort of falling off the cliff backwards. There was no sign of fear on the Native American's face though.

Though David was indeed momentarily transfixed, he recovered quickly.

"Fucking Idiot. Looks like those morons who dive off of cliffs in Mexico. He probably breaks his neck but lives and then calls me so he can sue somebody. Minority too so he'd probably win."

David then notices at the base of the painting the word "TRUST." "Yeah, right," David mumbles and then drifts off to sleep with the sound of the roaring flames, the steady rain, the rushing river and visions in his mind of falling off of cliffs in total trust.

Lori heads straight for bed still sobbing over she doesn't know what. She opens her window and the sounds of the rain and the river give her no comfort. She feels so incredibly lonely and thousands of miles away from anything. "Maybe I should have stayed with my parents" she thinks to herself. "I'm just not ready to be alone yet."

She stares into the flames with eyes of confusion and emptiness. When her eyes drift upwards the powerful Native American leaping from the top of the Falls hypnotizes her. Primal sexual urges and a connection to this leaping man erase feelings of loneliness and despair. She sees the name TRUST at the bottom of the painting and falls asleep dreaming that she too has taken the leap but clinging to this strong fearless man.

John bops around his room in ecstasy. He throws open the window and sticks his head out into the rain. He lets himself get chilled and wet and stands naked in front of the inferno burning in his room. Standing in front of the fire he too sees the painting TRUST and thrills at the sensations of leaping from the top of the Falls. Even though he is just looking at a painting, he knows that ecstasy and the elation and feels it now. He climbs in bed with all the covers on and falls asleep with an excited quiver in his stomach at taking the big leap.

Liz is incredibly perceptive and is still thinking about Paddy and the impish mystery he displayed this evening. She follows his directions and opens the window. She climbs into bed and stares intently at the fire while listening to the rain and the river outside. The painting above the fireplace startles her. It is too bold, too daring and too frightening. Still, she lingers a moment and thinks "maybe..." but shuts off her light instead and buries herself under a mountain of blankets. Safely cocooned, she falls fast asleep.

Chapter 2

David is no longer in his room at the Fall City Inn. His dream has taken him to ancient times and he is the Executioner. Tall, powerfully built and formidable, he stands before throngs of thousands who await his one swift blow with an axe to the neck of the guilty man kneeling before him. David is the most powerful man in the land and his massive masculine body is draped in leather and steel. His face is hidden behind a black veil. As he raises his axe suddenly an onlooker has leaped onto David's stage and is attempting to remove David's veil.

David picks up the crazed man with one hand and tosses him back into the crowd. But now there are more on stage and reaching for his veil. More and more, they keep coming, tearing and scratching at him and hanging all over him. They have found his one weakness and his fear is overwhelming.

He leaps off the stage and all of them are chasing and clinging to him. Now they are demons, hideous monsters with cruel curved teeth and cold eyes. They tear his flesh and rip to shreds his leather garments. Now he is naked and bleeding with ragged shards of exposed flesh dropping to the ground. Running, running, running but he never lets them remove his veil. But now they are upon him and their weight has brought him to his knees. He feels weak and relaxes his grip on his veil and feels the demons about to tear it from his face when...

David screams like a wounded child and erupts from his sleep. His body is shaking and his bedding is completely soaked in sweat. He runs to the window and starts breathing in the cool night air in gasping breaths.

"Shit! No wonder he told us to open our windows. Fucking place. I should have stayed up late and worked on my new case. Think I'll go take a shower and get my paperwork out and try to take my mind off of this crazy nightmare. Fucking thing was so real. I can still SMELL those fucking beasts climbing all over me. I sure looked good in leather with all those muscles bulging out though."

But David was exhausted from his nightmare and quickly fell back asleep. And in an instant, was right back where he left off.

The demons ripped the veil from David's face and an intensely blinding light erupted from David's head. The demons disappeared and David could SEE. He SAW his daughter growing up, he SAW why he kept others at a distance, he SAW beauty and sadness, he SAW rapture and joy and indeed he SAW Life. And then he SAW his recently deceased father approach him and he SAW the bitterness dissolve between them in an instant. He journeyed onwards and SAW the wind in the trees, the wind in the fields and the wind in his daughter's hair. For the first time in his life he could SEE and he was in awe.

296

This dream he did not awaken from till morning and his journey of sight carried him through the night. He let the demons keep his veil.

Liz too left her room for a faraway place. Her sons were at Columbine High when the Columbine tragedy occurred and now she was back at Columbine planting bright colorful Daisies all over the school grounds. Her husband died of cancer back at Albuquerque General Hospital and there she planted acres & acres of sunflowers. Her father had died in a car accident in San Antonio and she returned to the crash site and planted thousands of showy Dahlias. Onwards and onwards she returned to the garbage and the tragedies of her life and planted flowers. And they grew like no flowers on Earth. The immortal fuel that powered these flowers was now buried in a sea of blinding color. It was as if the past had been altered. No longer would Liz see the despair and the fear but instead would see what a fertile field she had planted for herself.

An intense and vivid dream, it would carry Liz on a journey from conception to present day and all in one long transformative night.

Phantoms from the portals of death clouded Lori's dreams. She drove cars at breakneck speed without brakes or steering. Mountains were being climbed by thousands of people but she couldn't take the first step. Ice, she kept falling backwards on the ice. And then she was floundering in the middle of the ocean with no land in sight. Sickly looking dogs were circling her and then she was trapped in a building with people chasing her and no way out. Up and down stairs, elevators, from room to room and no way to get out. Running hard, looking over her shoulder, sweating with fear and then...

Lori awoke with a start. The dreams of oppression and running and confusion were overwhelming her night after night. She was losing weight and a sleep deficit was accumulating and starting to wear her out.

She grabbed some blankets and crawled down on the floor next to the fire. She glanced up again at the Native American and saw no confusion and no fear in his face and wished that she had those qualities in her. She stared at the flames and they lulled her back to sleep.

But, for the first time, her dreams were marked not by confusion and fear but by an oozing serenity. She was. There were no words to describe it. She was. A stranger without a face walked up to her in her dream and said "Who are you?" and Lori answered "I am." And then she thought that perhaps she was like a simple sponge just soaking up information, senses, emotions, sights, sounds, smells and with no feelings and yet pure feelings. No judgments, just pure love. This land of "suchness" and "isness" is so different from my world she thought and quickly decided it was better than her world of fear and confusion.

Onward her dream carried her into realms she never had known before and she was simply basking and bathing in it, her fear and confusion magically gone.

John, the steelhead fisherman, often had dreams about fish, fishing and water and tonight was no exception. Tonight he was on a river of dreams wading the river under a heavy gray sky. In the shallows he spots a large Chinook salmon wallowing in the shallows where it is trapped. The fish is too big to get back into the main current and the dropping river is further stranding it. John walks over & gives the big salmon a boost back into the main current and the salmon then bursts upstream. But, partway up, the salmon stops swimming and rises out of the river and turns around to face John. The salmon suspends himself in midair and then silently thanks John with a flip of his fin. John then silently says "you're welcome" and the salmon drops back into the river and tears upstream pushing a 3 foot high wall of water.

John proceeds to find more and more stranded salmon, all separated from each other and stranded because of dropping water levels. One by one he helps the salmon back into the main current and more silent "thank yous" and "your welcomes" are exchanged.

And then John does the most amazing thing. He takes off all his clothes and enters the river and proceeds to swim upstream with the salmon. He feels his whole body come alive. His body is powerful and he feels the broad strokes of his tail propel him upstream though rapid waters. His belly brushes against rocks and he uses his fins to turn on a dime. He is a nasty mean male with long teeth and a cruel curved snout and he slashes at any other male that comes near him. He enjoys being a part of the throngs of fish heading upstream but also knows that his purpose is individual and singular.

As David sees the world for the first time, as Liz is planting flowers in the garbage dumps of her life and as Lori is just Being, John is swimming upstream with the salmon in a dream that is full of rapture and gratitude.

Fall City. A very precious downloaded book that I never completed. Today, after eighteen long years, I read the story not with revulsion but instead with happy sad tears of gratitude.

116

The Spectrum of Dreams

I love dreams, and to this day, it appears that most of my dreams are glimpses into "me," the many parts of me, and the many patterns that live *through* me. In short, most of my dreams seem to be just "regular" dreams. But there is also so much more. They still relate to me but in a more broad and expansive way.

Here's my "Spectrum of Dreams" as I have experienced them (note that I presented some of these dreams earlier in the book):

COLLECTIVE DREAMS: Collective dreams might be thought of as large collective movements taking place in consciousness that involve entire nations or even the Earth itself. As discussed earlier, an example of this might be the dream I had right after Trump was elected where I saw thousands of people lining the streets and cheering the Return of the Witch. I took this to be Life's balancing aspect—that if Trump represents a large collective movement toward patriarchal nationalism that the "witch" might be constellating in a large collective way to bring balance. Movements such as the return of the Angry Woman and Me Too Movement might be examples of this.

OUT-OF-BODY DREAMS: These are dreams in which I find myself some other place entirely experiencing events that are actually happening (while the body sleeps). Early one morning while dozing in bed, I had a profound dream experience of standing waist deep in the ocean at dawn in Southern California when a small earthquake hit. I could feel the odd sensations of the earthquake and shifting sand under my feet. I woke up and was so surprised that it was a dream. But I was even more surprised to find out later that day that an actual earthquake took place at that exact same time in Southern California! I know! I was there!

PRECOGNITIVE DREAMS: These are the sneak peeks and glimpses into the future showing actual people and events that take place later. I dreamed that an employee at work had a daughter who was engaged to be married to a big dude from Texas. I cautiously related the dream to my employee, who insisted that her daughter had no boyfriend. But a month later, the employee shows me a photo of her daughter with the big dude from Texas! It was him! And a few years later, they were married.

COURSE-CORRECTION DREAMS: These are dreams that suggest a new course of action. For example, occasionally dreams show up with a guide who is speaking to me and telling me what to do. One guide came in the form of Jesus who suggested I stop fighting so much—that it wasn't my "True North." (I loved to argue, and I loved competition, so this has not been an easy transition for me!) In another, I had been experiencing a long period of anger in my life when Brugh showed up in a dream to guide me. I watched him enter an outhouse with a loaded gun. He says to me, "Now I have three choices. One: I can shoot my way out. Two: I can kill myself. Three: I can go deep."

DREAMS FOR OTHERS: These are dreams in which I am given information *for* someone else. I had a dream that a friend of mine needed to open a healing center in Tucson, Arizona. Interestingly, she related that she had similar dreams where a goddess was insisting that she do hands-on healing work on behalf of others. A staunch rational type, this was hard for her to step into. Perhaps the dream came to me as added confirmation beyond what her own dreams were telling her. She did finally step into energy healing and did it the rest of her life.

DREAMS OF INTEGRATION: These are dreams that show a new energy, archetype, or resource that is now available to me. Sometimes it would be people that I had shunned who, in my dream world, were asking to be accepted and forgiven. Sometimes things and people would show up in dreams and fly into my heart center—a nun, a mountain, my ex-wife, etc. Watching all these things—people, symbols, and archetypes—enter my heart chakra was, for me, the chance to appreciate them all and, in a way, *become* them all—resulting in my being more whole and more resourceful. As shared earlier, when I became enamored with Barbara, the Vedic astrologer who exuded integrity, the spirit of Barbara fused with me.

DREAMS OF VOICES: These are dreams usually of guidance with no visuals—just a voice. Sometimes I don't see anything at all in a dream, but a voice is clearly speaking to me and instructing me. Some little flowers once suggested I eat them (they were Bleeding Heart flowers) if I wanted to see nature spirits. On another occasion, a voice spoke to me about the writing process. It said, "Mine. Refine. Polish."

DREAMS OF BALANCE: Dreams sometimes show up as a balancing aspect when I have strayed too far in one direction. As shared earlier, I had a tendency to repeatedly place certain spiritual teachers and presidents on pedestals. But a great assortment of dreams gushed forth restoring balance and reminding me that even the "greats" were human with all manner of human fears and foibles.

DREAMS OF SEEING DEEPER AND BEYOND THE ORDINARY: These are dreams taking me deeper and seeing behind the various masks we all wear. I've had dreams of seeing white men who struggle with structure and order shapeshift/transform into Native Americans—which seemed to be telling me that they are more fluid and connected to nature and uncomfortable with structure and logic.

DREAMS AS ONGOING STORIES OR NARRATIVES: Having faithfully recorded my dreams for the last nineteen years, I can see a lot of the same characters in my dreams doing much the same things night after night—sort of like a long, ongoing soap opera. But then, occasionally, there will be a big shift in the usual interior story, and I've learned that these big shifts portend big shifts in my waking world as well. As shared earlier, I went ten years with a Black Jaguar as my animal totem/guide, and then the Black Jaguar placed me on the back of an elephant—which I called Wise Elephant. I never saw my Black Jaguar ever again. In so many ways it was the announcement of the beginning of an interest in teaching, in sharing, in elderhood, in wisdom, and in serving others.

DREAMS OF PAST LIVES: These are dreams wherein a past-life memory was being revealed. I had visions of seeing myself as a Druid priest. I dreamed repeatedly that I was a Mayan priest. In other dreams, I have seen myself as a Catholic priest.

DREAMS OF TUNING IN TO THE ENERGY OF A PLACE ON EARTH: These are dreams where I am tuning in to the history of a particular place on Earth. While touring Egypt I was stunned by the power and history of the place, and it came crashing into my dream world nightly with powerful Egyptian symbols like the obelisk, Sekhmet, and Egyptian kings and queens.

DREAMS OF HEALING: These are dreams in which I am shown what is going on with me that is causing physical or emotional pain. I had six straight years of severe chronic neck pain resulting from being rear-ended in a car accident. A dream came forth showing me why my neck was not healing. (The dream was of a monk pacing back and forth outside my house.) Brugh worked with me to show me that the dream showed I had a spiritual monk in me that wanted to take root in me but that somehow, I was blocking it. That I carried massive resistance in my neck. After two years of opening to this monk and trying to not be so darn resistant to everything, the neck pain was gone.

DREAMS AS WARNINGS: Sometimes dreams appear as a warning. Years ago, I entered group therapy in a group that was composed primarily of women. A dream came through with all the women in my group cautiously asking me if I wanted to peel shrimp with them. But they were warning me that peeling shrimp was not easy. Images of the shells being peeled off and the shrimp being eaten seemed to be showing me that the dream was warning me that a period of vulnerability was coming. It was! In other dreams I have been shown that the path I was on was a dead end and a relationship I was in was cold and that our ships were going in different directions. I wasn't always prompt about making changes as a result of these warning dreams, but they were always accurate.

DREAMS OF GRACE: These are dreams I come away from feeling graced. By *graced*, I mean that it feels like I am allowed to see or experience something special and rarely seen or experienced. I was meditating once and was but a witness to this profound love between the light inside my body and the light (aura) that surrounds my body. They were sending profound oozy love to each other back and forth in a slow-motion love affair. There seemed to be no "purpose," no practical "takeaway" to the experience. It just felt like grace. It still does.

DREAMS OF UNITY: Sometimes dreams show our fundamental unity. In one dream, I was seated in a raucous noisy football stadium with fans for both sides screaming loudly. But suddenly, time stopped and every single person in the stadium had transformed into a piece of rose quartz lit from within by a beautiful pink light. In that moment, all the fans from both sides were in a timeless unity.

DREAMS OF DESTINY: These are dreams showing an individual a big picture vision of where life is headed. It may be short on specifics but more of a general vision of where one's ship is headed throughout the entirety of one's life. Brugh himself related the story that a dream in early childhood told him that he was going with Christ and that his family would not be joining him. He also related that a dream told him that at age thirty-five everything would change in his life. It did. I'm grateful for having my own destiny dream of what I called "Cosmos Man"—a walking embodiment of Love and Wisdom—many years ago and it still guides me today.

DREAMS OF EARTH: I have had many experiences in dreams that seemed to be showing me all about Earth as a living being. I was shocked once to see in a vision that Earth has a soul much like we do, and in another, I saw Earth praying.

DREAMS OF DREAMS: These are dreams where I am dreaming and realize I am in a dream. I had a dream once where I was in a dream and realized I was in a dream and since I was up and about, I wanted to see who was dreaming the dream since I was awake! What a shock it was to see a young woman in my bed asleep dreaming. What a shock this was because it seemed to be saying that "I" was not dreaming my dreams and that perhaps someone else in me is dreaming my dreams. As if dreams are not confusing enough!

DREAMS OF BOOKS NOT WRITTEN: Others have shared stories about seeing books in their dreams that had not actually been written yet. Or perhaps books written in consciousness and not in our actual physical world. As discussed earlier, gorgeous books appear in my dreams with captivating titles: *Unmistakable Life, Surrender to Freedom, The Real Descent,* and others—and the color, style, font, covers, etc. seem perfectly chosen. Are these "downloads" of information or perhaps a prodding from the universe to write them?

DREAMS FROM BOOKS: It is said that books carry an energy or frequency that can cause a dream or vision. In my case, it is often converted into a dream. Countless times, I have been reading books and suddenly needed a nap, and a powerful dream would come through related to the author and subject material.

DREAM QUALITIES: There are many different qualities to dreams. People who dream a lot and pay attention to them quickly discern that dreams seem to exist at many different levels. There are "regular" dreams and super-vivid high-definition Technicolor dreams. There are dreams where the dreamer seems to just witness a dream and dreams where a person is the actor in the dream and dreams where both are happening simultaneously. There are lucid dreams where one knows of the dreaming and seems to be able to direct the dream. There are dreams where the dreamer wakes up and just swears, "No way that was a dream! It was SO REAL!"

So that's my own experiences with my spectrum of dreams. Many of the categories overlap, but it is helpful to me to see that sometimes a dream is so often more than "just a dream."

When they come, those rare dreams and rare mystical encounters beyond a "normal" dream feel like just so much grace. I am eternally grateful to Brugh for opening the mystical dream doorway so that I might step through it. No matter how bad my day might have been, I always looked forward to seeing what might show up in my dreams. (I was sharing all these dreams with a friend of mine once who said, "Geez, John, if I had all those crazy dreams I might not ever get out of bed!")

I am also eternally grateful to Brugh for introducing me to the heart center as this place of unconditional love and unconditional compassion that is freely available to everyone. It has been tremendously supportive of my mystical journey and allowed me to greet the most beatific and most frightening images and experiences with a sort of infinite gratitude and appreciation. When I saw Bhagavan Das, I was struck by his love for his guru even though Das is now in his seventies. Though I choke a bit on the term *guru* (as I imagine most Westerners do), my gratitude for meeting Brugh and working with him many years ago has never wavered.

It sometimes seems that I have become a random accidental mystic dreamer and that the wide spectrum of dreams sometimes creates almost as many questions as there are answers, but my life is immeasurably richer because of them.

117

Kundalini—My Take

When the Kundalini energy first exploded through my body with unexpected hot pleasure in my hotel room in Philadelphia in 2004, I was both elated and frightened. The stranger the energetics became, the more I oscillated between feeling great grace and experiencing bouts of great fear. This compelled me to run and buy books to learn more about Kundalini energy, and also to discover books that would comfort me through reading about the experiences of others.

If I were to summarize the books I've read on Kundalini, it would be something like this: The Kundalini energy (the feminine principal called Shakti) lay dormant in most people's bodies and looks like a small serpent coiled up at the base of the spine. When awakened, it rises up through all of the chakras, purifying them along the way, and then it meets the masculine principal (Shiva) in the crown where they enjoy union.

But in an effort to stay true to my own experience, my own insights and my own observations, I would say that for me, it felt more like this:

Crazy and intense energy assaulted my entire body. There was the ascending energy up through the central channel from the root to the crown, and my dreams were most definitely of a feminine nature and were *full* of things like all manner of goddesses and serpents—especially cobras. (Good thing I am not afraid of snakes!)

But the energy was also exploding into my heart from outside of me, crashing into my kneecap, entering my palms, and flowing across my chest—and sometimes crushing me and exploding into my heart with shocking pain.

So, as to the energy itself, my description would be that there was a lot of it, all over the body, and far more than just energy ascending through the central channel along my spine.

About four years into the process, the crazy Kundalini Shakti energetics slowly began to fade. Then came phase two: The descent of light deep into the body. This is a beautiful and awe-inspiring thing to witness. Gorgeous white light from above descends all the way down to the root chakra and takes hold there.

What this light is, I can't exactly say, but it began erasing all my old desires, hobbies, and passions. My bucket list began to shrink. And shrink. And shrink. Until there was nothing. Dispassion. Waiting. Emptying. Endless letting go and surrendering.

Some describe this descent of light as *soul* and that more soul had entered my physical body. Some might say it was a whole new blueprint for me since light, at its core, is code. Some might call it *God*. Some might call it *love*. Some might call it *divinity*.

But what it felt like to me was that this beautiful white light was crowding out the old John while slowly and simultaneously anchoring someone new.

Prior to this descent of light, I recall having a vision of the crown of my head being wide open—like a gaping hole. I saw what looked like a serpent made of light yet with the qualities of water swirling above me, and this serpent of light was poking his head down just a bit as if checking things out with great care and caution. Maybe a week later came the massive descent of light.

So, my grand conclusion is that Kundalini Shakti does not necessarily rise up the central channel and meet Shiva in the crown and forever enjoy union there. My own experience was that the Kundalini Shakti prepares the body to hold and contain greater spiritual light. Perhaps she is the body, he is the light, and they work together. Maybe she is the form, and he is the blueprint.

What I learned from my experience with Mother Mary entering my body in 2005 was that the energetic vibration of divinity is far too great to be experienced within the human body for long. But perhaps if the human body were first upgraded, it could handle the extra power. That extra power feels like ecstatic love.

I know that the felt experience of the peace, bliss, joy, and love of one's divinity can be realized, felt, and experienced outside the body—such as in deep meditation. But to do it consistently inside the human body requires a major body upgrade, remodel, and rewiring first!

I'm not sure if this remodel of the human body ever truly ends. For the last fifteen years, I have learned to go with the flow with respect to my body. I still lift weights, mountain bike, swim, and hike, and I have five acres of yard to maintain. I generally stay very active. But every couple of months or so I must slow way down. I have days where I wake up, and my body feels like it weighs 1,000 pounds. I have no energy and just have to chill—usually just for a day but sometimes for a full week. Then I'm back to normal.

I suspect I am not alone and that millions of others are experiencing unexplainable energetic downloads and bodily upgrades entirely unrelated to aging or illness. I feel that there has never been a more important time for humankind to be kinder to their bodies and to take good care of them with better diet, regular exercise, quality sleep, and stress reduction.

Some say the soul of planet Earth is also going through an upgrade and that she herself expects humanity to join her in this new higher vibratory state. If so, perhaps we will all be experiencing these "ascension symptoms" on a regular basis.

What *is* this new higher vibratory state? At present, I can only guess. But, in my case, it feels like a nice balance between masculine and feminine. Every single thing one might use to describe masculine qualities and feminine qualities seems to exist in me in a sort of balance. I still rely more on my masculine qualities—they are comfortable and familiar to me, and sometimes I still get stuck there. But not for long.

Indeed, this may be where Earth is headed. No more patriarchy. No more matriarchy. A balance. A working together. One not better than the other.

Spiritual teachers Eugena Oganova and Isabelle Lambert have focused on coming changes for humankind here on planet Earth. They say that a new balance between our inner and outer King and Queen (sometimes called the electric/masculine polarity and the magnetic/feminine polarity) is indeed afoot on Earth. The old way looked like this:

- KING: Arrogance, Competition, War, Violence, and Judgment
- QUEEN: Manipulation, Scarcity, Victimhood, Apathy, and a do-it-*for*-me attitude

According to them, the new healthy King and Queen of the future will look like this:

- KING: Support, Patience, Cooperative Strategies, and Responsibility
- QUEEN: Love, Connectedness, Wisdom, and Pleasure

The two working together, achieving far more and discovering far more and experiencing far more and enjoying far more than in working alone. At present, this seems to be the result of the Kundalini energy in me—a nice and healthy balance between masculine and feminine, electric and magnetic, King and Queen.

118

Love and Synchronicity

Throughout all the changes and transformations and learning from new experiences in my life, there was and is love. And somehow it seems to me like the more one can love the human journey—all of it—the more doors seem to open in unexpected and miraculous ways that I like to call synchronicity.

What is it like to experience synchronicity?

It is the impossible coincidences that seem to happen over and over, seemingly beyond all statistical probability. It's a bit like being a gambler on a continuous streak of good luck. It's like someone out there is supporting you. This support and these "coincidences" are full of great joy and meaning. The more they are noticed, the more they occur. It feels like a connection to one's own soul, and in fact the yearning to be in alignment with the soul (and therefore with God) begins to grow and grow, and this creates even more of these miraculous events. They feel like grace. They feel like gifts from God. And once trusted, they happen more and more.

What would I tell others who desire their own experiences of synchronicity?

I would tell them to ask with sincerity that they would like to be in full alignment with their soul and their highest wisdom and to know that their soul is always connected to God.

I would tell them to do their best to find a way to love the entire human journey. All of it. Find a way to appreciate it all and be grateful for it all. Even if they get stuck in great anger and fear and grief and depression and guilt and shame—it's OK. When they are ready, try later to move to love and gratitude and appreciation for the experiences and ask what they learned from them.

Feel it all.

Allow it all.

Appreciate it all.

Love it all.

Glean wisdom from it all.

Then move on.

Last, I would suggest that everyone go deep inside and ask themselves, "What is it that I *truly* want and desire?" Trust that following one's very deepest desires will open unimaginable doors. Be vigilant about discovering the deepest desires, as sometimes the deepest desires are buried under enormous fear, resistance, and judgment.

It's not that hard to ask with sincerity to be in one hundred percent alignment with the soul (and therefore God). But be prepared, life may drastically change!

But loving the journey? *All* of it? That can be incredibly difficult. That's where the gift and grace of unconditional love in the heart center comes in.

This is an exercise that I use regularly:

Place your hands over your heart center with reverence (your heart center is located about an inch above where your ribs come together in the center of your chest). Call in to yourself unconditional love. Call in compassion. Call in healing. Call in harmony. And *allow* it all in. For yourself. Feel it. Be it. Return here as often as you like. Your free will can volitionally choose to see and experience life differently—in this case, through the eyes of unconditional love and the grace of the heart center. Try it! It's free! It's healthy for you and your body! Be sincere. Be patient. And see if you don't begin to see and feel and experience life working *for* you in strange, joyful, and miraculous ways.

Following desires can be easy.

While shooting a movie in England, Michael Crichton went to have readings done by psychics every day after his workday day was done. He was curious. He wanted to learn more. One of them said that Michael was psychic. Michael blew it off—only to find out much later that he was indeed very psychic. A door was opened that used to be closed when Michael followed his desire to sit with psychics.

Machelle Small Wright had never met a psychic before but followed her desire to meet with one. This same psychic suggested that Machelle start meditating. She did meditate daily for two years, which opened her up to quite literally talking and conversing with nature. Out of that, she created a garden she called Perelandra—an entirely new way of gardening and co-creating with nature.

Steve Jobs said that when he dropped out of college, he stopped taking the classes he *had* to take and instead took the classes he *wanted* to take. One class he wanted to take was a calligraphy class, and it was that calligraphy class that gave him an appreciation for typography. Because of that class, Jobs did something really new—he added many different fonts to choose from in the Macintosh computer, making it unique and putting Apple on the map.

Following the little threads of desire can lead to unexpected and synchronistic miracles if there is the courage to listen to those desires and to see where they lead.

Align the self with the soul, and with the highest wisdom.

Choose to experience life through unconditional love.

Follow the absolute deepest desires, no matter how large or how small.

See where they lead.

I will meet you there. I will be there, waiting.

Love to All!

119

Still a Work in Progress

I'm lying in bed. I can feel many beings standing over me. One of them says to the others:

"He is still a work in progress."

The journey is enthralling. And humbling.

Acknowledgments

Immense and heartfelt thanks to my wife Wendy for your essence of support. I feel blessed to share my deep love for you and I am grateful for the forces that brought us together. I so appreciate our life of love and synchronicity together.

Thank you to my parents David Latta and Kay Latta for giving me the gift of life.

To my son Eric Latta and my daughter Kelsey Latta. I am grateful to be your father and thankful for the life experiences we shared together. And thank you Kelsey for helping me design the cover of this book!

Thank you to my original editorial, book formatting, and book design team of Carol Killman Rosenberg and Gary Rosenberg. You are the best Book Couple ever!

Many friends took their precious time to review the early manuscript and offer their thoughts, reviews, and insights. Thank you!

Carolyn Conger. Thank you so much for your love, wise guidance, and soul support.

Thanks to all my Brothers worldwide in the Mankind Project.

And infinite gratitude to Brugh Joy. The Heart Priest who so humbly and selflessly shared an ocean of transformational unconditional love and wisdom with me that has forever changed my life.

About the Author

John David Latta is a mystic, author, teacher, and founder and CEO of a multimillion-dollar consumer products company. He shares intimate and personal stories and teaches workshops on healing, transformation, awakening, love, synchronicity, and wisdom that unite and expand human experience. He lives with his wife, Wendy, in Redmond, Washington. Visit him at www.johndavidlatta.com.

For more great books visit Empower Press online at
Books.GracePointPublishing.com

If you enjoyed reading *The Synchronicity of Love* and purchased it
through an online retailer, please return to the site and write a
review to help others find this book.